40 Power To

Can Make

135798642

ISBN 10: 1-933502-20-7   ISBN 13: 978-1-933502-20-5

Originally published in 1941

Linden Publishing Inc.
2006 S. Mary
Fresno CA
www.lindenpub.com
800-345-4447

10-in. TABLE SAW

Features

Takes a 10-in. blade,
which raises, lowers, tilts
Has built-in sawdust chute
Large 30 by 40-in. table
Cuts 2½ in. deep with
a 10-in blade

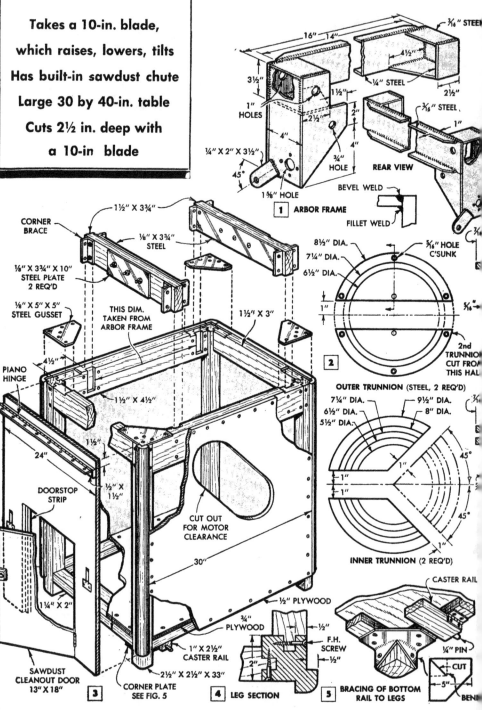

1 ARBOR FRAME

BEVEL WELD
FILLET WELD

2 OUTER TRUNNION (STEEL, 2 REQ'D)

INNER TRUNNION (2 REQ'D)

3

4 LEG SECTION

5 BRACING OF BOTTOM RAIL TO LEGS

HAS TILTING ARBOR

By Elman Wood

Part I

WOODWORKING craftsmen will rate this tilting-arbor table saw "tops" because of its versatility, speed and accuracy. By turning one handwheel the blade is raised or lowered for any depth setting within its capacity. A few turns of another handwheel tilt the blade for any angle cut up to 45 deg., the settings being indicated by a degree scale and pointer. The saw table remains always in a horizontal position; only the saw arbor tilts. The hardwood table with hinged extensions is plenty large enough to handle a 4 by 8-ft. plywood panel. An enclosed base catches all the sawdust, and swivel casters fitted to built-in foot lifts enable the operator to roll the saw to any part of the shop.

Construction should begin with the saw-base frame, Fig. 3. Building the base requires care in cutting and fitting as it must be strong and rigid to support the motor and arbor assembly. Use well-seasoned, selected oak for legs and rails. Rabbet the legs on adjacent sides as in Fig. 4 to take side and end panels flush. Both top and bottom rails are mortised into the legs, but note that the upper side rails are 4½ in. wide and that the end ones are 3 in. The tenons are glued and keyed with screws, and after the joining is completed, steel gussets are mortised into the

Hinged side and back extensions increase the size of the table so that the ripping fence can be set 25 in. from the saw blade. Rips to the center of 48-in. plywood panel

top rails across the four corners, and the bottom rails are braced to the legs with steel corner plates cut, bent and attached as in Fig. 5. Caster rails, one across each end, are hinged to the underside of the

An accurate scale with pointer shows all angles from 0 to 45 deg. Here blade is tilted to full 45-deg. angle

Saw frame and arbor assembly completed ready for the table. Base is painted before table is installed

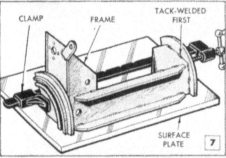

CLAMP FRAME TACK-WELDED FIRST

SURFACE PLATE **7**

frame rails as in Figs. 3 and 5. The plywood bottom and the rear and right-side panels can now be installed, but the front and left-side panels are omitted at this stage as it is necessary to determine later the location of the handwheels and the size of the opening for the motor.

The arbor frame, shown in front and rear views in Fig. 1, comes next. This consists of a number of parts cut from steel plate and welded together to form the unit shown. This frame swings on trunnions made as detailed in Fig. 2. Each trunnion consists of an inner and outer segment, the two trunnions requiring four segments in all. These four segments are obtained from ¾-in. mild-steel plate turned first to the form of disks, which are then cut into segments as indicated in Fig. 2. Inner segments are welded to the arbor frame while the outer ones are attached to the steel-faced cross members in Fig. 3. In installing a trunnion-mounted saw arbor there are two precise requirements: The center line of the blade must coincide exactly with the center line of the outer trunnion segments and the center of rotation of the trunnions must be at that point where the plane of the blade intersects that of the saw-table top. Fig. 6 shows the arbor and arbor frame in position and Fig. 7 shows the first step in positioning the inner trunnion segments on the arbor frame. Use a surface plate or other flat surface and make sure that the parts are exactly in line before welding. This done, measure the length of the arbor frame, plus the four trunnion segments. This gives you the distance between the two trunnion-support members, Fig. 1. Face the members with steel plates as

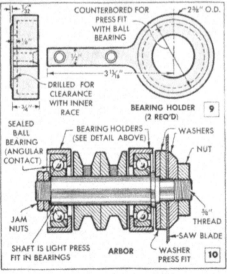

COUNTERBORED FOR PRESS FIT WITH BALL BEARING
2⅜" O.D.
½"
3¹³⁄₁₆"
DRILLED FOR CLEARANCE WITH INNER RACE
BEARING HOLDER **9** (2 REQ'D)

SEALED BALL BEARING (ANGULAR CONTACT)
BEARING HOLDERS (SEE DETAIL ABOVE)
WASHERS
NUT
⅝" THREAD
SAW BLADE
JAM NUTS
SHAFT IS LIGHT PRESS FIT IN BEARINGS
ARBOR
WASHER PRESS FIT
10

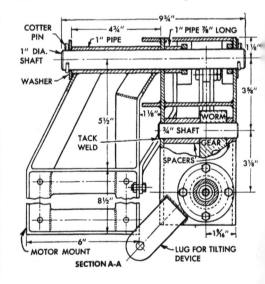

9¾"
COTTER PIN
4¾"
1" PIPE ⅞" LONG
1" PIPE
1⅛"
1" DIA. SHAFT
WASHER
5½"
TACK WELD
1⅛"
WORM
¾" SHAFT
GEAR
SPACERS
3⅝"
3⅛"
8½"
6"
MOTOR MOUNT
1⅛"
LUG FOR TILTING DEVICE
SECTION A-A

4

shown and drill the bolt holes. While the members are temporarily in position determine the center line of the saw base and scribe it on both members for guidance in locating the trunnions. Then slip the arbor frame and trunnions between the supports. The arbor frame should fit snugly but should swing on the trunnions with only a slight frictional drag. With all parts located on the center line of the saw base, clamp the outer trunnion segments to the cross members and lift out the whole assembly. Using each trunnion segment as a drilling jig, drill holes and bolt the segments to the cross members.

Next come the arbor bearing holders shown in detail in Fig. 9, and in section in Fig. 10, with the arbor, pulley and bearings in place. Holders are rough-cut from ¾-in. steel plate with a cutting torch or metal-cutting bandsaw and are recessed and bored through to suit the bearings as in Fig. 8. Bearings should be a fairly tight press fit in the recesses. The arbor or spindle is machined from steel and finish-ground to final dimensions. Note that it is flanged at the saw-blade end to form a seat for the press-fitted spacing washer. The spindle is shouldered and threaded at the left-hand end for jam nuts for pre-loading the bearings. Pulleys are locked on the spindle with socket-head setscrews, the ends of the setscrews seating on a flat, milled or filed on the saw spindle. Dimensions of the spindle through the bearings, Fig. 9, and also the bearing-recess diameter in Fig. 10, have been

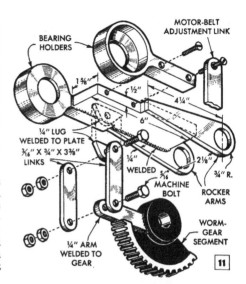

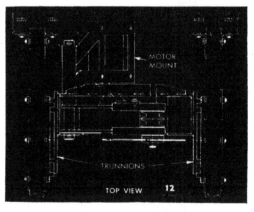

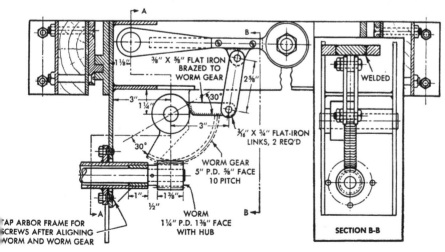

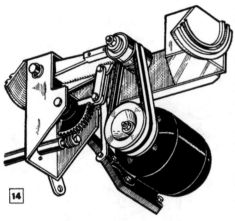

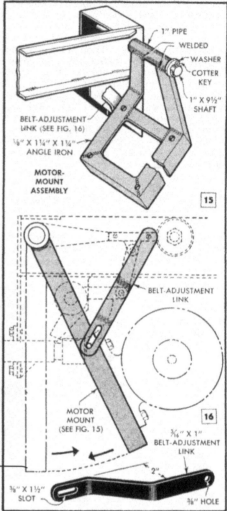

purposely omitted. These measurements must be taken from the bearings at hand.

Now, before going further, study carefully sections A-A and B-B in Fig. 13, also the perspective and top views in Figs. 11 and 12. From Fig. 11 you will see that a ½-in. steel plate forms the mounting base for the saw-arbor assembly. Notches milled in opposite edges take the ends of the bearing holders, and rocker arms welded to the mounting base allow it to pivot on a rocker shaft for raising and lowering the saw blade and motor as a unit. When this assembly is complete, the saw spindle should turn freely in the bearings. Check this before finally welding the bearing holders in place. The motor mount, a separate assembly built up by welding together steel angles and flats, is welded to a length of 1-in. pipe which telescopes over the rocker shaft and fits snugly against the rocker arms. See Fig. 13, section A-A, and also the top view, Fig. 12. Shaft, pipe sleeve and arbor mounting are held in place in the arbor frame by washers and cotter keys. When assembled, the parts should move freely but without any end play. The motor mount is not fully dimensioned as it must be made to fit the base of the motor you are to use. Final unit in this assembly is the belt-adjustment link, Figs. 15 and 16. It's made from flat iron, bent to approximately a 2-in. offset and drilled and slotted as indicated. Upper end is bolted to the left bearing holder, Fig. 12, and the lower end to the motor mount. Loosening the lower bolt allows the motor to be moved up or down to obtain correct belt tension.

The raising-and-lowering mechanism consists of a worm and worm-gear segment, the latter made from an ordinary gear by simply cutting away all but a 120-deg. segment. An arm made from ¼-in. flat iron is welded or brazed to the segment as in Figs. 11 and 13. This arm is connected to

a lug welded to the underside of the arbor plate by two links as shown. The gear segment turns on a shaft passing through the sides of the boxed end of the arbor frame as in Fig. 14. The shaft is made a drive fit in the holes drilled in the frame. Spacers cut from pipe position the worm-gear segment on the shaft, as shown in Fig. 13, section A-A. Although not detailed, the raising mechanism will operate more smoothly if the gear segment is fitted with a bronze bushing. If this is done, the bushing should be a tight drive fit in a reamed hole. Fig. 13 shows worm and worm shaft in position.

¶A set of socket wrenches can be made by using the heads of hexagon socket screws and welding handles to them.

10-in. TABLE SAW HAS TILTING ARBOR

Part II

By Elman Wood

WITH THE SAW completed to the stage described in Part I, the assembly is ready for installation of the arbor-tilting mechanism, Fig. 17. Here the handwheel drives the tilting screw through miter gears which are 1½-in. pitch diameter, 12 pitch, 18 teeth with a ⁷⁄₁₆-in. face. A frame, assembled from flat iron, supports the hand-wheel-shaft housing and the miter-gear drive. As will be seen from Fig. 17-A, this frame consists of two angle brackets and one straight support piece, the latter mortised into the leg of the frame. Both the larger angle bracket and the flat support are slipped over the ends of the handwheel-shaft housing, bolted temporarily in place and checked for alignment. Then the pipe housings are tack-welded to the brackets in the positions shown in the sectional view, Fig. 17-A. Bolts and screws hold these two parts in place when the assembly is made. Notice that the second angle bracket forms a frame for positioning the miter gears and that it pivots on the projecting end of the handwheel-shaft housing, Fig. 17-A. It is held in place by the driving miter gear,

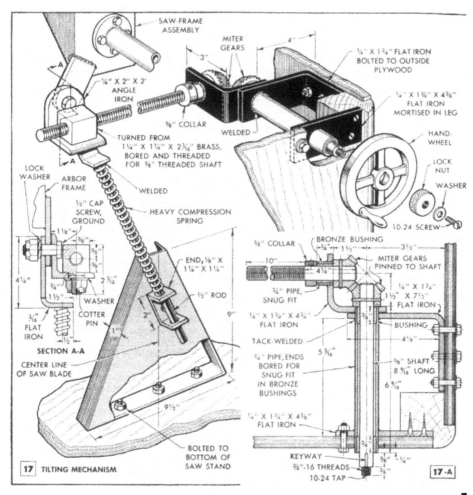

17 TILTING MECHANISM

17-A

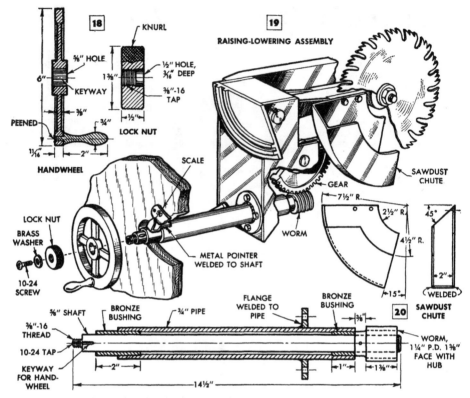

18 HANDWHEEL

⅝" HOLE
6"
KEYWAY
⅜"
PEENED
11/16"
2"

KNURL
½" HOLE, 3/16" DEEP
1⅜"
¾"
⅜"-16 TAP
½"
LOCK NUT

19 RAISING-LOWERING ASSEMBLY

SCALE
LOCK NUT
BRASS WASHER
10-24 SCREW
METAL POINTER WELDED TO SHAFT

GEAR
WORM
7½" R.
2½" R.
4½" R.
45°
15°
2"
WELDED

SAWDUST CHUTE

20 SAWDUST CHUTE

⅝" SHAFT
BRONZE BUSHING
¾" PIPE
⅜"-16 THREAD
10-24 TAP
KEYWAY FOR HAND-WHEEL
FLANGE WELDED TO PIPE
BRONZE BUSHING
⅜"
WORM, 1¼" P.D. 1⅜" FACE WITH HUB
2"
1"
1⅜"
14½"

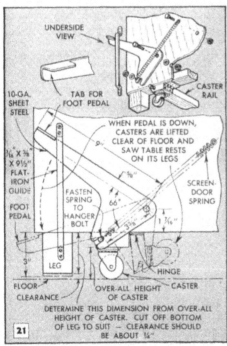

21
UNDERSIDE VIEW
10-GA. SHEET STEEL
TAB FOR FOOT PEDAL
CASTER RAIL
⅜" X ⅜" X 9½" FLAT-IRON GUIDE
FOOT PEDAL
WHEN PEDAL IS DOWN, CASTERS ARE LIFTED CLEAR OF FLOOR AND SAW TABLE RESTS ON ITS LEGS
SCREEN-DOOR SPRING
FASTEN SPRING TO HANGER BOLT
66°
3"
LEG
HINGE
CASTER
FLOOR CLEARANCE
OVER-ALL HEIGHT OF CASTER
DETERMINE THIS DIMENSION FROM OVER-ALL HEIGHT OF CASTER. CUT OFF BOTTOM OF LEG TO SUIT – CLEARANCE SHOULD BE ABOUT ¼"

which is pinned to the handwheel shaft. Likewise, the driven gear is pinned to a threaded tilting shaft. Pivoted in this way the shaft and gears can swivel with the arbor frame when it is tilted to any angle up to 45 deg. The tilting shaft is threaded with a ⅝-11 thread.

The tapped block, into which the threaded tilting shaft turns, is bolted to an angle bracket that pivots on the tilting lug welded to the arbor frame. This end of the tilting assembly is carried on a spring-loaded toggle supported by a triangular metal bracket bolted to the bottom of the saw stand as in Fig. 17. The toggle partially supports the weight of the motor and arbor through the 45-deg. tilt and thereby eases the load on the tilting handwheel. The toggle-spring guide rod is welded to an angle bracket bent from flat iron and bolted to the tilting lug as in section A-A, Fig. 17. Handwheels and knurled lock nuts for both the raising-and-lowering and the tilting mechanisms are detailed in Fig. 18. Both are keyed to the shaft in the same way, Figs. 17 and 19.

The worm shaft and housing, not fully described in Part I, is detailed in Fig. 19. It is similar to the tilting-gear shaft and

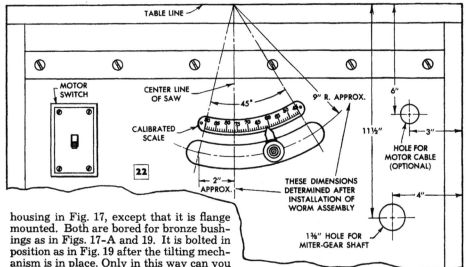

TABLE LINE

MOTOR SWITCH

CENTER LINE OF SAW

45°

9" R. APPROX.

CALIBRATED SCALE

6"

11½"

3"

HOLE FOR MOTOR CABLE (OPTIONAL)

22

2" APPROX.

THESE DIMENSIONS DETERMINED AFTER INSTALLATION OF WORM ASSEMBLY

4"

1⅜" HOLE FOR MITER-GEAR SHAFT

housing in Fig. 17, except that it is flange mounted. Both are bored for bronze bushings as in Figs. 17-A and 19. It is bolted in position as in Fig. 19 after the tilting mechanism is in place. Only in this way can you determine the exact dimensions and location of the curved clearance slot in the front panel of the saw base, Fig. 22. The best way to determine the exact location of the curved slot and the location of the hole for the miter-gear shaft in the front plywood panel, is first to assemble the tilting mechanism, as in Fig. 17, with the flat support plate attached to the leg with screws, as shown. This will support the completely assembled mechanism in place. Then it is easy to determine the location of these openings in the front panel. After the slot has been located and cut and the hole for the miter-gear shaft has been bored, the panel is screwed permanently in place.

The calibrated scale, Fig. 22, can be made from thin sheet metal with figures and divisions stamped into the metal by hand with a numeral stamp of the type used for stamping numerals on tools. For stamping the divisions, a ¼-in. lathe bit ground to a blunt chisel edge will do. The degree scale must be laid out very accurately, and care should be taken when stamping not to cut

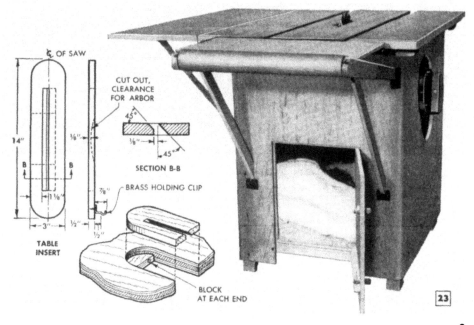

¢ OF SAW

CUT OUT, CLEARANCE FOR ARBOR

45°

⅛"

⅛"

45°

SECTION B-B

14"

⅛"

B   B

BRASS HOLDING CLIP

1¼"

⅞"

3"   ½"

½"

TABLE INSERT

BLOCK AT EACH END

23

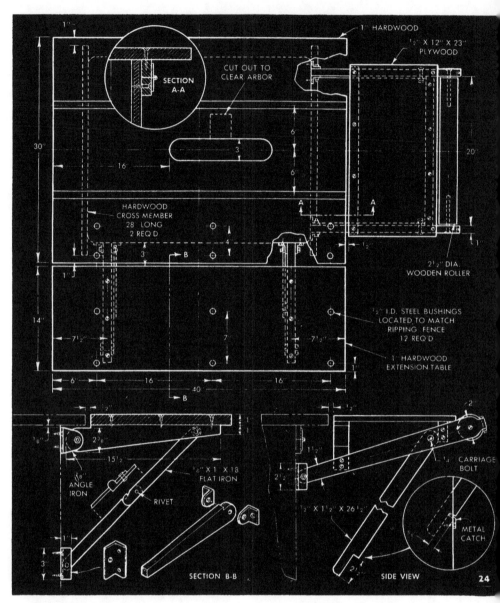

SECTION A-A

CUT OUT TO CLEAR ARBOR

1" HARDWOOD

½" X 12" X 23" PLYWOOD

30"

16"

HARDWOOD CROSS MEMBER 28" LONG 2 REQ'D

14"

7½"

7½"

6"

16"

40"

6"

16"

20"

2½" DIA. WOODEN ROLLER

½" I.D. STEEL BUSHINGS LOCATED TO MATCH RIPPING FENCE 12 REQ'D

1" HARDWOOD EXTENSION TABLE

2⅜"

15½"

ANGLE IRON

RIVET

⅛" X 1 X 18 FLAT IRON

SECTION B-B

1½"

2½"

½" X 1½" X 26½"

CARRIAGE BOLT

METAL CATCH

SIDE VIEW

24

the numerals or divisions through the metal. To make the scale easy to read, coat the face with black enamel and allow to dry. Then follow with a thin coat of white. Wipe this off immediately with a single quick sweep of a dry cloth. This will remove all the white enamel except that in the indentations. After the enamel has dried, locate the 45 and 90-deg. positions of the saw blade and position the scale accordingly. Attach it to the panel with small screws. Cut a pointer from heavy-gauge sheet metal and weld it to the worm-shaft housing as

in Figs. 19 and 22. The sawdust chute, detailed in Fig. 20, is optional, its only purpose being to direct dust and chips to the rear of the enclosed base. If you do include the chute, make it from heavy sheet metal, welding where indicated in Fig. 20. Bolt it to the arbor frame in the position shown in Fig. 19 and be sure to allow for ample clearance when the saw is tilted 45 deg.

The table can be made from 1-in. plywood, but it is better to build it from strips of 1-in. hardwood doweled and glued. The most attractive job is made by gluing up alternate 1 by 1-in. strips ripped from hardwoods of a contrasting color. Otherwise, using one wood such as maple, dowel and glue together 1-in. strips, each no wider than 2 in., to make the required table width as given in Fig. 24. Make the extension drop leaf in the same way and of the same material. After gluing, run grooves for the crosscut guide and cut an opening for the blade insert as in Fig. 24. Make and fit the insert as detailed in Fig. 23. Attach the table to the base as in Fig. 24, section A-A, checking to assure that the crosscut-guide grooves are aligned with the blade. Fig. 24, section B-B, shows how the side extension is mounted on the saw base. The back extension, Fig. 24, is optional equipment.

Use a regular crosscut guide or make one as in Figs. 25 and 26. Details on the hardwood ripping fence, Fig. 27, are self explanatory. Casters detailed in Fig. 21 also are optional. The lifting mechanism for each set of casters is fitted on diagonal corners of the base.

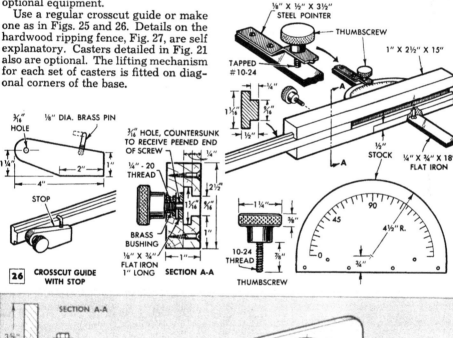

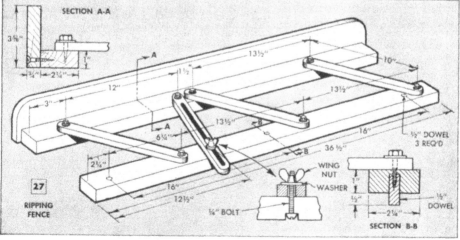

10-in. Self-feeding

① LEFT SIDE

② FRONT

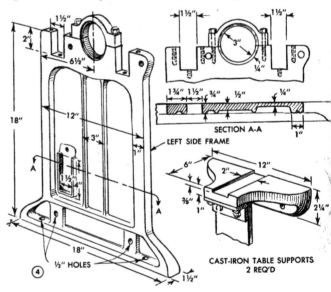

③ RIGHT SIDE

CABINETMAKERS, builders, furniture-repair shops and home craftsmen will find plenty of use for this homemade thickness planer. It's fitted with all the accessories commonly supplied on a bench machine of this type, including the conventional 3-knife cutterhead, safety chip breaker and automatic power feed. It will surface stock up to 10 in. wide, from ¼ to 4 in. thick, and any convenient length.

Fig. 7 details assembly of the cutterhead and the gear drive to the feed rolls. Feed-roll gears are each 6 in. in diameter with 48 teeth. The gears are driven by a 14-tooth pinion which in turn is driven by a 60-tooth sprocket chain driven from a 10-tooth sprocket on a countershaft. As shown in Figs. 1 and 5, this sprocket takes its power from a V-belt-drive reduction on the opposite side of the machine. With a 1750-r.p.m. motor use drive pulleys of a size to give the cutter head a speed of 3600 r.p.m. Then calculate the size of the V-pulley reduction to give feed rolls a speed of 40 r.p.m.

Construction of the planer begins with the frame members, one of which is detailed in Fig. 4. These parts are cast right and left hand, pads being provided on the right-hand member as in the top view, Fig. 7. Only the outer side of each is recessed and webbed. This simplifies the making of the wood pattern from which the parts are cast. In making the pattern don't forget to allow 3/32 to 1/8 in. for shrinkage of the casting on all dimensions. This is the correct shrinkage allowance for cast iron. Note in Fig. 4 that the bearing caps must be cast separately. Seats for the cutterhead bearing cages, Fig. 6, are machined with the caps in place. Remainder of the fitting can be done with files or a hand grinder.

In-feed and out-feed rolls are carried in floating bearings which are spring-loaded by means of the arrangement shown in detail in Fig. 7. The bearings are milled from cast iron or cold-rolled steel, bronze brushed, and are provided with flanges which act as guides. A fillister-head cap screw in the

SECTION A-A
LEFT SIDE FRAME

CAST-IRON TABLE SUPPORTS
2 REQ'D

④ ½" HOLES

THICKNESS PLANER

By P. A. Messinger

upper face of each bearing holds the lower end of the compression spring in place. The in-feed roll is grooved or fluted so as to grip the surface of the stock and feed it uniformly under the cutterhead. This job can be done in a milling machine at your local machine shop for a nominal charge. Figs. 6 and 12 give the necessary dimensions for machining the cutter head, another job for the local machine shop. Have the knives, pressure bars and setscrews at hand before machining the head so that if necessary the measurements can be varied slightly to suit. Knives, or blades, should be the conventional type of high-speed steel. Note that the holes in the pressure bars, Fig. 12, are tapped at an angle and that the knife is tightened in place by turning the setscrews out. At least four screws should be used in each of the three pressure bars and they must be located exactly equidistant. Bearings must be a snug push fit on the cutterhead shaft. The detail in Fig. 6 shows how the head is mounted in the frame. Bearings are mounted in cages with oil seals

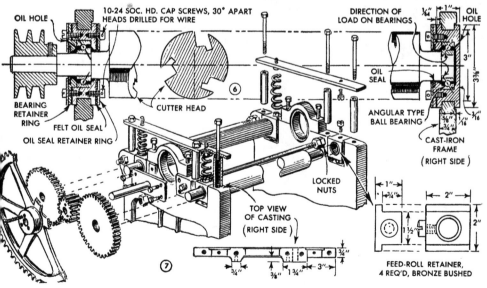

OIL HOLE

10-24 SOC. HD. CAP SCREWS, 30° APART
HEADS DRILLED FOR WIRE

DIRECTION OF
LOAD ON BEARINGS

OIL
HOLE

OIL
SEAL

3"

3⅜"

BEARING
RETAINER
RING

FELT OIL SEAL

CUTTER HEAD

OIL SEAL RETAINER RING

ANGULAR TYPE
BALL BEARING

CAST-IRON
FRAME
(RIGHT SIDE)

LOCKED
NUTS

TOP VIEW
OF CASTING
(RIGHT SIDE)

FEED-ROLL RETAINER,
4 REQ'D, BRONZE BUSHED

1"

¾"

2"

1½"

2"

¾"

¾"

¾"

1¾"

3"

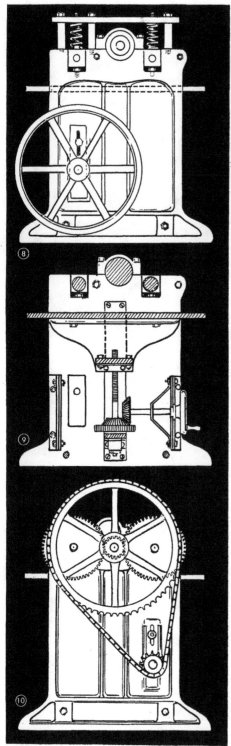

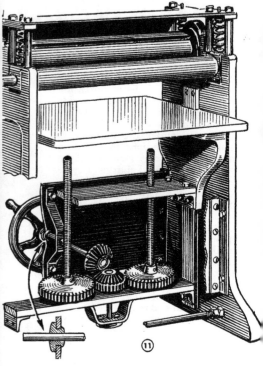

and bearing retainers and provision is made for lubrication. Notice that the heads of the inside cap screws are drilled transversely so that they can be wired. The frames are held together by four ½-in. tie rods with locked nuts on both sides of each frame member, Fig. 13. In this position they act as adjustable spacers and in the final assembly, because of the angular-type ball bearings on the cutterhead, care must be taken that the adjustment is exact.

The table is made from ½-in. cast iron or ¼-in. steel plate, 12 in. wide and any convenient length. Cast-iron supporting brackets are dimensioned in the lower-right detail in Fig. 4, and the complete table assembly is shown in Fig. 11. The table slides up and down on flat steel guides, ½ by 2 in. in sectional size. The adjusting mechanism, Figs. 9 and 11, is operated by a handwheel and consists of two rods, threaded right and left hand, each ⅝ in. in diameter and 6 in. long. Each screw turns into a hole tapped in a horizontal steel bar. A spur gear on the lower end of each screw engages a pinion, which is driven by a bevel gear actuated by the handwheel. This arrangement turns both screws simultaneously, thus raising or lowering the table with a uniform slow motion. A scale and pointer can be mounted on the table and frame to indicate the exact depth of cut.

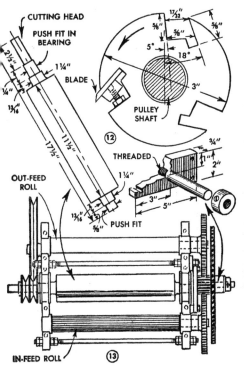

CUTTING HEAD

PUSH FIT IN BEARING

$2\frac{1}{2}$"

$1\frac{1}{4}$"

BLADE

$\frac{1}{4}$"

$\frac{13}{16}$"

$17\frac{1}{2}$"

$11\frac{1}{2}$"

$\frac{17}{32}$"

$\frac{5}{16}$" $\frac{5}{16}$" $\frac{5}{16}$"

5° 18° 3"

PULLEY SHAFT

⑫

$\frac{3}{4}$"

THREADED

$1\frac{1}{4}$"

$1\frac{1}{4}$" 2"

3" 5"

OUT-FEED ROLL

$\frac{13}{16}$" $\frac{5}{16}$" PUSH FIT

IN-FEED ROLL ⑬

⑭

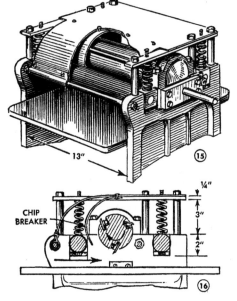

13" ⑮

CHIP BREAKER

$\frac{1}{4}$" 3" 2"

⑯

Like the feed-roll bearings the counter-shaft bearings are of the floating type, riding in slots cast in the side frames, Figs. 4, 8 and 10. Tension of the V-belt and roller chain holds the bearings against slotted adjustment members, Figs. 8 and 10. This arrangement provides for easy adjustment of the tension on the belt and chain drives. Bearings should be a close, sliding fit in the slots so that there is no side play. This will mean some hand filing to assure a perfect fit. In assembling, make sure that all rotating parts turn freely with no binding at any point. See that the table raises and lowers easily but without any looseness in the slides. Then tighten all locked nuts on the spacer studs uniformly.

The chip breaker and top guard or cover, Figs. 15 and 16, are made of heavy sheet metal and fitted in the positions indicated. The chip breaker and guard also serve as a deflector for chips and any slivers that may be raised by the cutterhead. The stream of chips is thus thrown to the rear of the machine. The handwheel on the original planer, Fig. 14, was taken from an old sewing machine but any small hand-wheel or ball crank will serve the purpose. As in the left-side, front and right-side views, Figs. 1 to 3 inclusive, the finished planer should be mounted on a heavy, rigid base made of hardwood joined with bolts. The base can be fitted with small metal truck wheels and folding handles. For light work a $\frac{3}{4}$-hp. motor is sufficient, but for heavy continuous work, a 1-hp. or larger motor is necessary. One precaution will save a lot of knife sharpening. Keep a stiff-bristle brush handy and give each piece of stock a thorough brushing before running it through the machine. This is especially helpful on old or used lumber.

15

Cutoff Saw Hung From Ceiling Pivots For Various Cuts

both ends of the shaft extend through the plates, you can use them by simply turning down the shaft so that the bearing can be moved in to allow for the saw. In assembling the mandrel, the plates are bolted

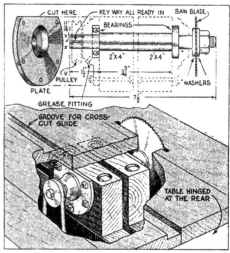

to blocks on the underside of the saw table as indicated, being sure that the plates are in perfect alignment to avoid binding.

Here's a simple cutoff saw that anyone can assemble. The novelty of this setup is that the front axle of an old car is used. This is suspended from the ceiling or basement joists. The saw mandrel is attached to the lower end of the axle and the motor is mounted on a shelf supported by a flat-iron bracket near the upper end of the assembly. Loosening the axle nut at the ceiling permits the saw to be turned for making a cut at almost any angle across the work without moving the latter.

Saw Mandrel Made Inexpensively From Generator Parts

A ball-bearing mandrel for a homemade circular saw can be assembled at little cost by using the armature shaft from an old car generator. The pulley end of the shaft and end plate of the generator housing can be used without alteration. The other end of the shaft will have to be turned down to take the saw blade and to fit the bearing in the end plate of another generator. If

Guides Permit Filing Bandsaw In Ordinary Saw Vise

The addition of these guides to the ends of the stationary jaw of your saw vise converts it to hold a bandsaw blade. Drill

and tap both ends of the jaw so that rectangular pieces of sheet metal can be pivoted to them to support the blade at the correct height above the jaws.

16

Power CORDWOOD SAWS *you can build*

By W. C. Lammey

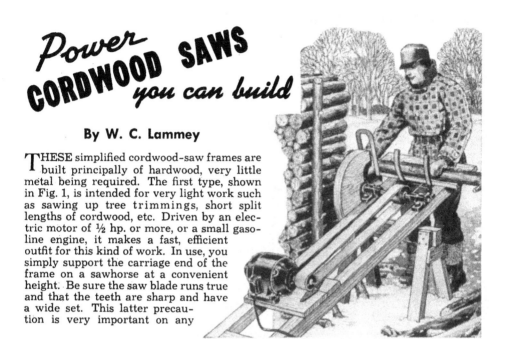

THESE simplified cordwood-saw frames are built principally of hardwood, very little metal being required. The first type, shown in Fig. 1, is intended for very light work such as sawing up tree trimmings, short split lengths of cordwood, etc. Driven by an electric motor of ½ hp. or more, or a small gasoline engine, it makes a fast, efficient outfit for this kind of work. In use, you simply support the carriage end of the frame on a sawhorse at a convenient height. Be sure the saw blade runs true and that the teeth are sharp and have a wide set. This latter precaution is very important on any

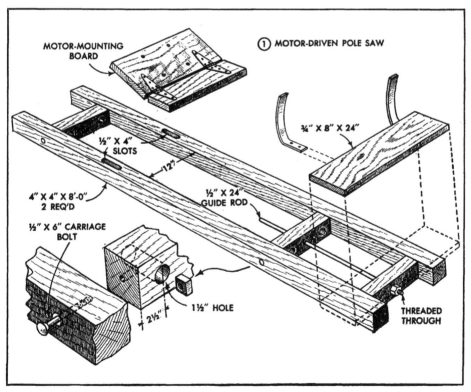

MOTOR-MOUNTING BOARD

① MOTOR-DRIVEN POLE SAW

¾" X 8" X 24"

½" X 4" SLOTS

12"

4" X 4" X 8'-0", 2 REQ'D

½" X 24" GUIDE ROD

½" X 6" CARRIAGE BOLT

1½" HOLE

2½"

THREADED THROUGH

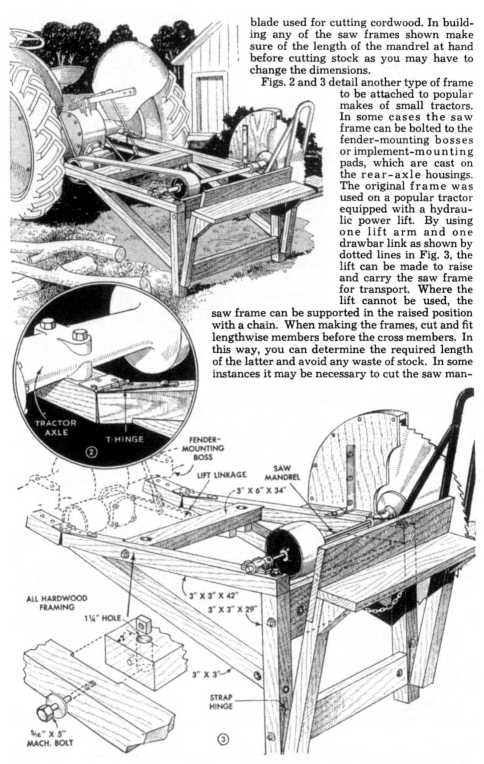

blade used for cutting cordwood. In building any of the saw frames shown make sure of the length of the mandrel at hand before cutting stock as you may have to change the dimensions.

Figs. 2 and 3 detail another type of frame to be attached to popular makes of small tractors. In some cases the saw frame can be bolted to the fender-mounting bosses or implement-mounting pads, which are cast on the rear-axle housings. The original frame was used on a popular tractor equipped with a hydraulic power lift. By using one lift arm and one drawbar link as shown by dotted lines in Fig. 3, the lift can be made to raise and carry the saw frame for transport. Where the lift cannot be used, the saw frame can be supported in the raised position with a chain. When making the frames, cut and fit lengthwise members before the cross members. In this way, you can determine the required length of the latter and avoid any waste of stock. In some instances it may be necessary to cut the saw man-

TRACTOR AXLE

T-HINGE

②

FENDER-MOUNTING BOSS

LIFT LINKAGE

SAW MANDREL

3" X 6" X 34"

ALL HARDWOOD FRAMING

1¼" HOLE

3" X 3" X 42"

3" X 3" X 29"

3" X 3"

STRAP HINGE

⁵⁄₁₆" X 5" MACH. BOLT

③

drel to suitable length and have it machined for some distance back from the pulley end so that the pulley can be placed between bearings as in Fig. 3. Be sure that the end of the mandrel shaft does not project more than ½ in. or so beyond the bearing. A projecting shaft end is dangerous as it may catch loose clothing.

A stationary frame for heavier work is detailed in Fig. 4. Although not shown, skids easily are added to this frame if desired. If the mandrel is fitted with a balance wheel, the distance between bearings will be shortened from that shown, and the width dimensions of the frame will have to be altered accordingly. Although it takes somewhat more time to join the frames with the type of bolted joints detailed, the method has the advantage of rigidity and durability. Moreover, if the wood shrinks and the joints loosen, the whole frame can be tightened.

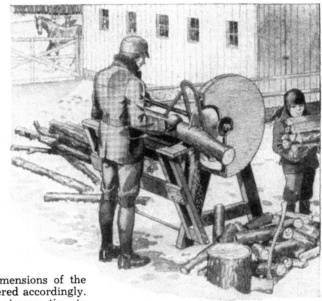

Figs. 5, 6 and 7 show a frame which, with some minor adaptation, can be fitted to the front of almost any tractor having side frames that ordinarily are used for attaching implements. Note that when the saw

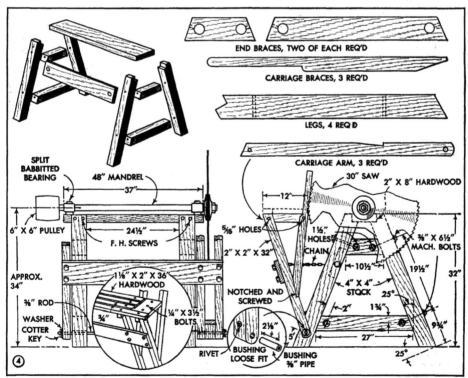

19

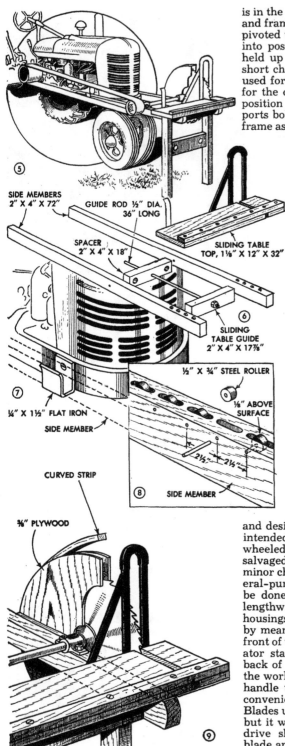

SIDE MEMBERS
2" X 4" X 72"

GUIDE ROD ½" DIA.
36" LONG

SPACER
2" X 4" X 18"

SLIDING TABLE
TOP, 1⅛" X 12" X 32"

⑥

SLIDING
TABLE GUIDE
2" X 4" X 17⅞"

½" X ¾" STEEL ROLLER

⅛" ABOVE
SURFACE

⑦

¼" X 1½" FLAT IRON

SIDE MEMBER

2½" ← → 2½"

⑧

SIDE MEMBER

CURVED STRIP

⅜" PLYWOOD

⑨

is in the operating position, Fig. 5, the table and frame are supported on legs, which are pivoted to the frame and swing downward into position. For transport, the legs are held up against the frame by means of a short chain or hook. Hardwood should be used for the legs and 2 by 6-in. hardwood for the crosspiece. When in the transport position the frame rests on U-shaped supports bolted to the front end of the tractor frame as in Fig. 7.

Carriage tables that move horizontally can be provided with rollers if desired. Fig. 8 suggests a simple way of fitting these rollers under the carriage. Disks ½ in. thick are cut from a piece of ¾-in. steel shafting with a hacksaw and center-drilled to take a 10d nail loosely so the roller will turn on the nail. Holes are bored and slots chiseled in the frame piece to take the rollers as indicated. A strip of flat iron screwed to the bottom of the carriage board will make a suitable "track." Use hardwood for all frames, and finish with two coats of spar varnish or implement paint to protect the wood. Fig. 9 shows a simple and effective saw guard made from a piece of plywood and screwed to the frame back of the blade. A curved strip is screwed to the plywood edge just outside the circle of the saw teeth. Such a guard does not interfere with removing the blade, yet offers protection against one of the greatest dangers to the operator of a cordwood saw, that of a sliver or small piece of wood or other object falling on the blade when it is running.

Fig. 10 shows a cordwood saw similar to a swinging cutoff saw and designed for heavy work. This saw is intended for mounting on a truck or four-wheeled trailer and can be driven with a salvaged automobile engine. With some minor changes it can be mounted on a general-purpose tractor also. This usually can be done by bolting the rear ends of the lengthwise frame members to the rear-axle housings and supporting the forward ends by means of a cross member bolted to the front of the tractor frame. In use, the operator stands between the frame members back of the saw and swings the blade into the work. The table is stationary. Helpers handle the logs which can be cut to any convenient length for several men to carry. Blades up to 36 in. in diameter can be used, but it will be necessary to shift the upper drive shaft so that the larger-diameter blade and the mandrel will clear the table.

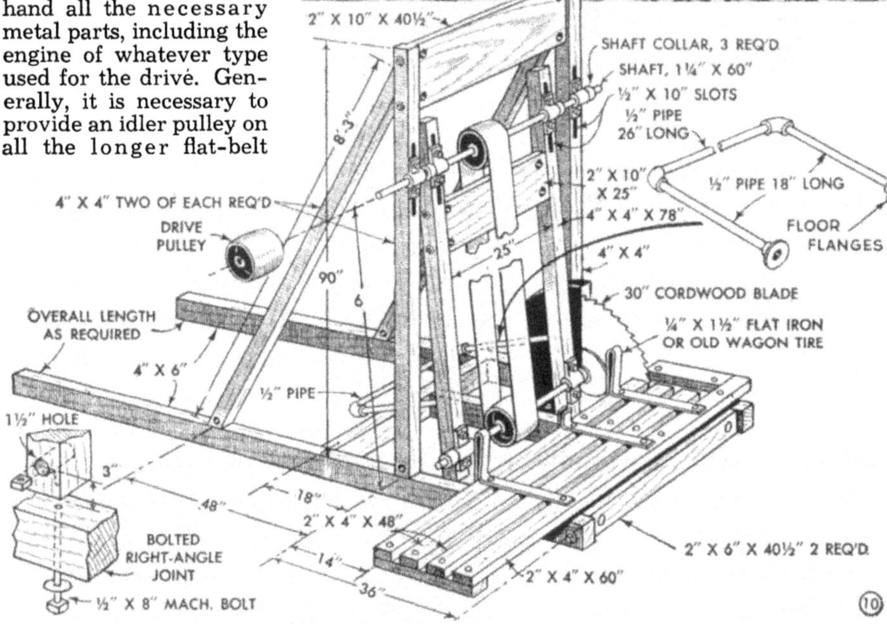

If you use different size blades, an adjustable stop should be provided. All shaft bearings should be provided with pressure grease fittings. Only certain of the dimensions are given on the frame. Changes necessary to adapt the design to use of salvaged pulleys, shafting and other parts must be left to the builder as dimensions must be changed to suit what one has at hand or can obtain. Some machining usually has to be done on the saw mandrel to adapt it to use with this design. Don't cut any valuable stock or timbers until you have at hand all the necessary metal parts, including the engine of whatever type used for the drive. Generally, it is necessary to provide an idler pulley on all the longer flat-belt

2" X 10" X 40½"
SHAFT COLLAR, 3 REQ'D
SHAFT, 1¼" X 60"
½" X 10" SLOTS
½" PIPE 26" LONG
4" X 4" TWO OF EACH REQ'D
DRIVE PULLEY
2" X 10" X 25"
½" PIPE 18" LONG
4" X 4" X 78"
FLOOR FLANGES
4" X 4"
OVERALL LENGTH AS REQUIRED
90°
25°
30" CORDWOOD BLADE
¼" X 1½" FLAT IRON OR OLD WAGON TIRE
4" X 6"
½" PIPE
1½" HOLE
3"
48"
18"
2" X 4" X 48"
BOLTED RIGHT-ANGLE JOINT
14"
2" X 4" X 60"
36"
½" X 8" MACH. BOLT
2" X 6" X 40½" 2 REQ'D.
⑩

drives. The idler should run on the slack side of the belt nearest the driven pulley and just how it is installed depends on the type of idler and mounting you have or can obtain. When you mount the mandrel on any of the frames that are attached to the tractor, it's a good idea to provide slots so that you can shift it forward or backward. This will enable you to make the proper adjustment for table travel into the saw blade. And of course steel angles are better than wood for making almost any design of cordwood-saw frame.

Two final and important precautions:

Always make certain that the blade is tight on the mandrel before starting, and do not exceed the recommended speeds for the size blade you are using. As an example of the latter, the speed of a 30-in. blade should not exceed 1500 r.p.m. A speed of 1200 r.p.m. is safer, while larger diameter blades should run proportionately slower.

¶Grease-sealed ball bearings with a ½-in. hole make excellent collars for a shaper. Because this type of collar remains stationary, the usual burned mark is eliminated from the work.

Altered Auto Piston Forms Sturdy Grinder Head

With little alteration, an old auto piston can be converted into a grinder head for light work. The piston skirt is sawed off just below the wristpin bosses. Part of the remaining piston wall is then cut away to allow for the V-belt drive. By cutting a hole in the base of the grinder it can just as well be driven from underneath. The shaft is a cold-rolled rod with its ends turned down to fit the grinding-wheel holes and threaded for retaining nuts. Collars are made to hold the grinding wheel. The pulley is turned from steel and is held in place with a setscrew. Oil holes are drilled in the shaft bearings. After drilling screw holes in the base, the grinder is ready to fasten to the bench.

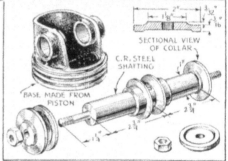

Two Shafts Held in Alignment While Transferring Holes

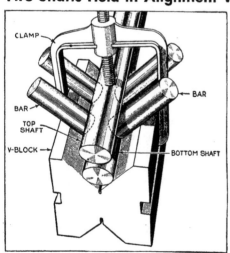

When it is necessary to hold two shafts, one directly above the other, for transferring or marking off drilled holes, the job can be done by using a V-block, a tightening clamp and four short pieces of round rod of slightly less diameter than the shafting. One of the shafts is laid in the V-block, two rods are placed on each side, as indicated in the illustration, and finally the top shaft is laid on these, after which the clamp is screwed down to keep the assembly firmly in position.

H. Moore, Leeds, England.

¶Nuts and bolts that are exposed to the weather may be prevented from rusting by applying a coating of asbestos roofing cement to the threads of the bolts before tightening the nuts.

DRILL-PRESS TAPPING ATTACHMENT

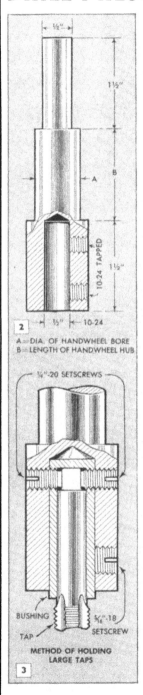

A = DIA. OF HANDWHEEL BORE
B = LENGTH OF HANDWHEEL HUB

METHOD OF HOLDING
LARGE TAPS

By Walter E. Burton

THIS ATTACHMENT makes a hand tapping machine of any small drill press. The unit utilizes the accuracy of the machine to guide the tap squarely into the hole, a trick that is quite difficult to do by hand with an ordinary tap wrench. Fig. 1 shows the unit in operation. By using the hand feed of the drill press and turning the tap with the large handwheel, a delicate feed is obtained which avoids tap breakage. No power is used, the tapping being done by hand.

To make the attachment, you need a true-running handwheel 8 in. in diameter, a length of 1-in. cold-rolled-steel shafting for the adapter, a key-operated chuck of ½-in. capacity, and several socket-head setscrews. The exact method of machining the adapter will depend on the type of spindle on the drill press and the method of mounting the tapping chuck. The adapter shown in Figs. 1 and 2 is attached to a drill-press spindle having a collar with a ½-in. hole and two setscrews for holding router bits, etc. It takes a drill chuck fitted with a ½-in. straight shank. Fig. 2 details the adapter for a straight-shanked chuck. It is machined all over and shouldered to three diameters. The hole drilled in the large end is reamed to finish diameter. Transverse holes are drilled and tapped for 10-24 socket-head setscrews. Machine the

23

ream the handwheel hub to a tight slip fit.

A key-type chuck like that shown is satisfactory for taps up to ⅜ in., but for larger taps a special chuck, Fig. 3, is needed. In construction, this is similar to the adapter shown in Fig. 2, except that it holds the tap by means of setscrews and bushings, several of which are made to fit varying sizes of taps. Notice that ¼-in. No. 20 setscrews turn into holes drilled and tapped through both the adapter sleeve and the bushing, Fig. 3. The setscrews seat on the squared end of the tap, making a positive nonslip drive. The detail shows a closed-end bushing, the closed end acting as a stop when the tap is inserted. This provision is handy on short-run production, but open-end bushings can be used, of course. Fig. 4 shows the three parts of the unit required for installation on the average drill press. Careful machine work is necessary as any misalignment will cause repeated tap breakage. Work must be mounted securely on the drill-press table and tap holes should be drilled with the drill press to assure accuracy.

other end of the adapter, Fig. 2, to a diameter of ½ in. for a distance of about 1½ in. This diameter will fit most drill-press spindles of the type shown. Drill and tap the handwheel hub for a ⁵⁄₁₆-in. No. 18 socket-head setscrew. File a flat on the middle section of the adapter to provide a seat for the handwheel setscrew, and then bore and

Pipe-and-Spud Guy Hitch Holds Fast in Marshy or Sandy Ground

When it is necessary to guy derricks, cranes or other equipment in marshy or sandy soil where it is impractical to dig a pit for a deadman, the hitch shown will effectively anchor the guy. This hitch is made from a length of 5 or 6-in.-dia. pipe with the ends left open to enable it to be driven into the ground. A spud about 2 ft. long is welded at a 60-deg. angle near the upper end of the pipe, and an eye for a turnbuckle hook is welded just above the junction of the pipe and spud. To use this

hitch, drive the pipe into the ground so that the spud is almost flush with the surface and rest the end of the spud on a short plank placed at right angles to the direction of pull. The pressure of the spud against the plank and the resistance of the lower end of the pipe to being forced backward, hold the hitch securely. One of the main causes of a hitch gradually working loose is the transmission of vibration from the guy to the hitch. This often can be remedied by using two hitches, as shown in detail A, with the turnbuckles adjusted so that their lengths are unequal. This method also is efficient if two ordinary iron stakes are used for the hitches instead of the special pipe-and-spud assembly.—Elton Sterrett, Houston, Tex.

Mandrel Expands to Hold Work

If you have a number of rollers or similar items to face, this expanding mandrel will permit them to be mounted and removed from the lathe

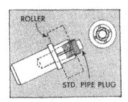

rapidly. Turn a shoulder on the mandrel to seat squarely in a 4-jaw chuck. Then drill, tap and slot end, as shown, to take a pipe plug. Tightening the plug after the work is mounted expands the end to hold the work.

POWER DRAG SAW

A small electric motor drives blade 100 strokes per minute, cutting logs up to 24 in. in diameter

By Edward R. Lucas

BUCKING LOGS and large limbs into cordwood or stovewood lengths by any hand method is a hard, time-wasting job no modern farmer or woodsman likes to think about. A power drag saw like the one pictured will do this work in less than half the time, and the only labor involved is moving the unit from one cut to the next.

The simple A-frame, Figs. 1 and 4, is made of 2 by 4-in. pine. Also, the base for the jackshaft and the foot at the narrow end of the frame are of the same material. Lower ends of the long frame members are cut at an angle of 15 deg. so that when attached, the foot will rest squarely on the ground. Both the crankshaft and jackshaft run in ordinary pillow-block bearings, and the shafts are held in position with collars. Construction of the pitman-drive assembly is detailed in Figs. 3 and 5, and side and top views are supplemented by sectional details A–A, B–B and C–C, which show the inner construction at various points. The crosshead carriage must be of the floating type to allow the saw blade free movement up and down. Crosshead guides are cut from ½-in. black pipe, this grade being used because it is easier to polish than galvanized pipe. Polishing is done by clamping the length of pipe in a vise—being careful not to crush it out of round—and first cutting off the paint and surface irregularities with a coarse abrasive cloth. Loop a strip of the cloth over the pipe and pull it back and forth. Polish in the same manner with a fine-grit abrasive strip 1 in. wide. Light oil makes abrasive cut cleaner.

Make the pivot block, section C–C, of

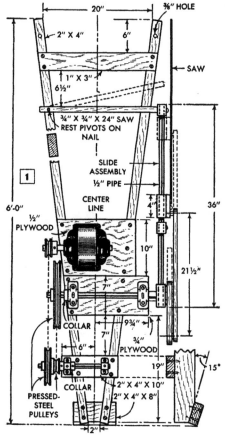

through the crosshead should be slightly oversize to give an easy, sliding fit over the guides. Sections A-A and B-B, Fig. 3, show the method of mounting the hardwood pitman. Both ends of the pitman are fitted with bronze bushings. The crank is laid out as in Fig. 3 and cut from selected hardwood. It is flange-mounted as in Fig. 4, section C-C, using a 4-in. V-pulley as the flange. Note that the pulley hub is pinned to the shaft with a transverse pin.

With all parts of the frame assembled and the drive and crosshead assembly in place, bolt the saw blade to the crosshead. Be careful to get the blade lined up with the crosshead guides so that it moves in a straight line. Finally, locate the crosshead-guide spacers in the clear and bolt in place as in Fig. 5. Drill a ⅜-in. hole near the end of each frame piece to take a ⅜-in. machine bolt. When the saw is set up for work, these bolts are driven into the log as in Fig. 2 to hold the unit in place. Back them out with a wrench when the cut is completed. Keep the blade sharp and give the teeth a medium-wide set. The pivoted saw rest, Figs. 1 and 4, is provided to support the blade when not in use. This is cut to swing under a hook as shown in Fig. 4.

hardwood such as oak and fit it with a ¾-in. bronze bushing, which should be a drive fit and located as in Fig. 5. Then make duplicate spacers of hardwood, Fig. 5, and drill these and the pivot block to take the pipe guides. In this operation, care must be taken to get the holes centered across the width of the blocks and exactly the same distance apart along the length. Holes

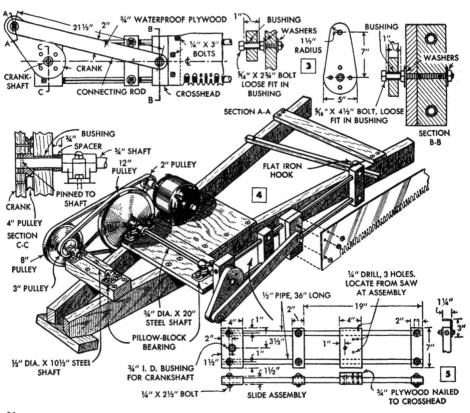

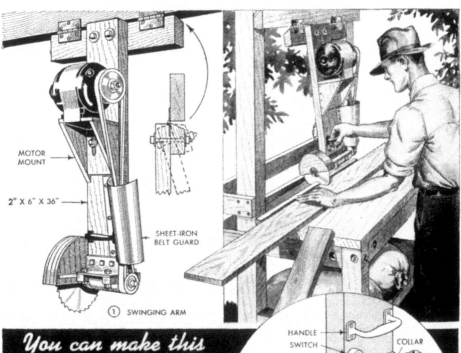

MOTOR MOUNT

2" X 6" X 36"

SHEET-IRON BELT GUARD

① SWINGING ARM

You can make this
SWING SAW

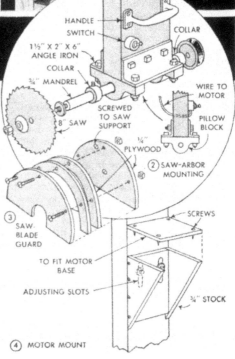

HANDLE
SWITCH
1½" X 2" X 6" ANGLE IRON
COLLAR
¾" MANDREL
8" SAW
SCREWED TO SAW SUPPORT
COLLAR
WIRE TO MOTOR
PILLOW BLOCK
¼" PLYWOOD
② SAW-ARBOR MOUNTING
③ SAW-BLADE GUARD
TO FIT MOTOR BASE
ADJUSTING SLOTS
SCREWS
¾" STOCK
④ MOTOR MOUNT

YOU'LL find a swing saw one of the handiest tools in your shop. Besides taking care of practically all sawing operations usually done on a small bench saw, it will handle wide or long work. With one hand pulling the saw and the other holding the work firmly against the fence, there is no reason for having your hands near the cutting edge. Also, the saw is safe in that it swings away from the operator by its own weight when released.

You can do crosscutting, mitering or ripping, Figs. 7, 8 and 9, by simply screwing suitable fences to the table. In ripping, the saw is locked in a vertical position with a suitable fence fastened to the bench to guide the work. Metal cutting is easily accomplished by using a cutting disk in place of the saw blade. Likewise, a sanding disk may be used on the mandrel for many disk-sanding operations. The capacity of the saw as

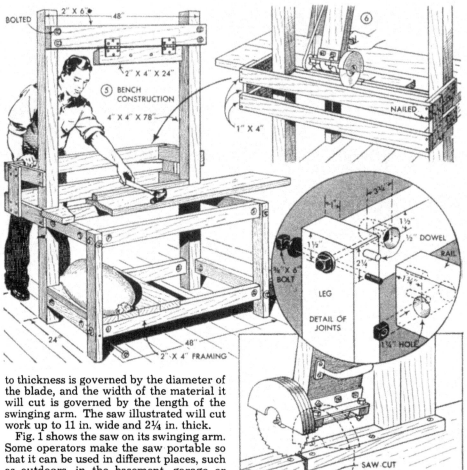

BOLTED
2" X 6"
48"
2" X 4" X 24"
(5) BENCH CONSTRUCTION
4" X 4" X 78"
1" X 4"
NAILED
(6)
24"
48"
2" X 4" FRAMING
3¾" X 6" BOLT
DETAIL OF JOINTS
LEG
1"
1½"
2¼
3¾"
1½
½" DOWEL
RAIL
1¾"
1¾" HOLE
SAW CUT
(7) SAW FENCE

to thickness is governed by the diameter of the blade, and the width of the material it will cut is governed by the length of the swinging arm. The saw illustrated will cut work up to 11 in. wide and 2¼ in. thick.

Fig. 1 shows the saw on its swinging arm. Some operators make the saw portable so that it can be used in different places, such as outdoors, in the basement, garage or other building, suspending the saw from a joist in the basement and using a special bench outside or in the garage. When the saw is made portable, large butt door hinges are ideal for suspending it. In this way, the saw can be released for moving by simply pulling out the hinge pins. The hinges should have snug-fitting pins to eliminate practically all play, and some means of locking the pins should be provided. You can readily understand what would happen if one of the pins should work out while the saw is in operation.

Notice that the 2 by 4-in. horizontal member of the swinging arm is beveled on the upper edge so that the saw can be pushed back past the vertical position. Fig. 2 shows the assembly of the mandrel and saw blade, and Fig. 3 shows the blade guard. The latter can be cut from ¼-in. plywood or hard-pressed board, and is assembled with stove bolts and screwed to the edge of the swinging arm. A toggle

switch is placed close to the handle on the arm so that the motor can be controlled without releasing the arm.

To prevent any possibility of injury from the belt, a sheet-metal guard should be provided. This can be shaped and attached as in Fig. 1. Whether or not the belt is crossed as shown will depend on the direction in which the motor rotates. Fig. 4 shows the motor mount. This is adjustable vertically for tightening the belt, the adjusting being done by loosening two bolts that slide in slots in the mount. After making an adjustment be sure the bolts are tight before operating the saw.

Construction of the special bench is given in Fig. 5. The circular detail at the right shows how the joints are assembled with bolts. This type of construction is desirable because bolts can be tightened to compensate for wood shrinkage, thus as-

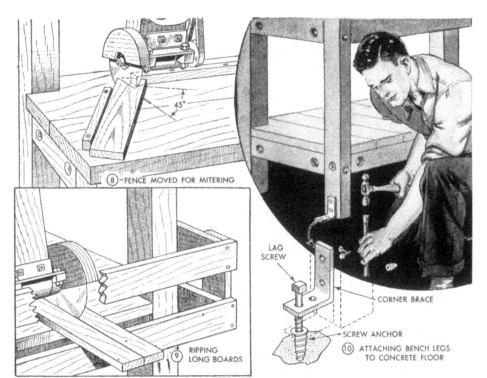

(8)—FENCE MOVED FOR MITERING

LAG SCREW

CORNER BRACE

RIPPING LONG BOARDS (9)

SCREW ANCHOR

(10) ATTACHING BENCH LEGS TO CONCRETE FLOOR

suring a rigid bench at all times. Although over-all width of the bench is given as 4 ft., it can be made any size desired. If you want to use the saw for cutting large sheets of plywood, make the bench accordingly, allowing room to install suitable fences. To prevent creeping or tipping, it may be necessary to provide some means of holding the bench. If it is desired to have the bench portable, a couple of large sandbags will do. But, where portability is not a require-ment, a better way is to fasten the front legs to the floor by means of corner braces or angle brackets. On a concrete floor, an-choring can be done as in Fig. 10, using lag screws held in expanders.

For safety's sake be sure to provide a rear guard on the bench. A simple one assembled as in Fig. 6 will prevent anyone from accidentally coming in contact with the saw. Be sure to locate it so that work can slide between the strips when ripping.

Lubricating High-Speed Drill

Many times the life of a high-speed drill is shortened because it was improperly lu-bricated. If a length of loose-fitting rubber tubing is placed over the drill when it is being used and oil is applied through the tubing, the drill will last longer. The lubricant that ordinarily is thrown off the drill by centrifu-gal force will drain down the inner wall of the tubing and flood the work at the point where it is needed.

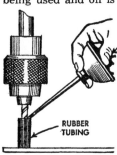

RUBBER TUBING

Small Ignition Wrenches Carried On Shower-Curtain Ring

Sets of small combination wrenches for ig-nition work are carried easily on a shower-curtain ring attached to your trouser belt. If you prefer not to carry them in this manner, the ring may be hung on a nail within easy reach of the work-bench or kept in a toolbox. A snap or key chain will serve the same purpose. Such a holder also is handy for carrying a small assortment of washers or nuts.

SHOWER-CURTAIN RING

29

Quick-on

DRILL-PRESS CLAMPS

By Will Thomas

These clamps are so designed that they drop into the slots in the drill-press table and can be tightened in a jiffy. They are especially handy when doing close work because it's never necessary to remove nuts and washers from bolts that project under the table. As you see in Fig. 1, the individual clamps can be set in various positions to hold work which is irregular in shape. Fig. 2 details one unit, and you can make as many as you need by simply duplicating parts and operations. To make duplicate clamps, chuck 1½-in. round cold-rolled stock off-center as in Fig. 4, carrying the outer end of the piece on the tail center. Turn to the dimensions given in Fig. 2 and you have four cam shapes as in Fig. 4. Saw these apart, then drill and tap for the clamping bolts, Fig. 3. The rectangular-shaped nuts, Fig. 2, are cut from ³⁄₁₆-in. flat steel and finished by filing. Be sure that the nuts slip through the table slots. Drill and tap nuts exactly in the center so that strain is equalized when the bolts are tightened.

CLAMPING BOLT ¼"-20 1¾" LONG

9/16"

5/16"

1¼"

3/16"

¼"-20 CAP SCREWS

5/16"

1¼" DIA.

HOLD-DOWN BOLT

3/16"

1"

NUT

TO SUIT TABLE SLOT

Clamps also can be used on a milling machine or lathe faceplate to hold irregular-shaped work

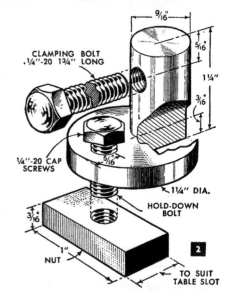

Make Your Own
HYDRAULIC PRESS

By E. S. Harris

FOR fitting bushings into connecting rods, forcing gears on shafts, removing axles from small wheels and similar work in the garage, service station or shop, a hydraulic press like the one illustrated will do the job quickly and efficiently. It consists of a hydraulic auto jack, some pipe and pipe fittings and a frame made from odds and ends of scrap iron usual-

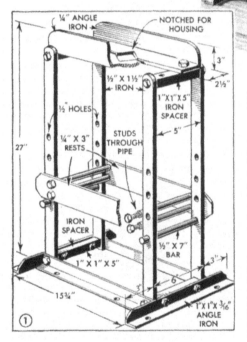

ly available at garages and machine shops.

Four pieces of angle iron forming the base are bolted to the workbench, and the uprights are attached with ½-in. bolts. Four spacers, shown in Fig. 1, are drilled and tapped for ½-in. bolts which hold them to the uprights. The top of the press is made from two lengths of angle iron which are bolted to the spacers. A notch is cut in each piece of angle iron through which the

jack will be inserted later, and two steel retaining blocks, similarly notched as shown in the circular detail of Fig. 2, are drilled and tapped for two ½-in. bolts on each side and on the underside to receive a similar bolt extending through the slot where the pieces of angle iron butt together. The adjustable rests are supported at any one of four positions by bars placed through ½-in. holes spaced at 3-in. intervals in the uprights, and are held together tightly by four studs running through sections of iron pipe.

The cylinder and piston of the hydraulic jack are removed as a unit, and a piece of round bar stock of the same diameter and length as the cylinder is substituted. A hole is drilled through it lengthwise for the passage of fluid, and the ends are threaded, one end to screw into the base of the jack housing, the other to take a nut and pipe reducer into which the feed pipe is to be fitted. After the bar is screwed into the housing, a washer is placed over it and the nut turned down tightly to prevent loss of fluid. It may be necessary to put a gasket under the washer as a seal. Instead of using a reducer, the feed pipe can be threaded and fitted into a counterbored, tapped hole in the bar.

Next, make a housing for the cylinder and piston. This is made from a length of 1¾-in. iron pipe about half as long as the

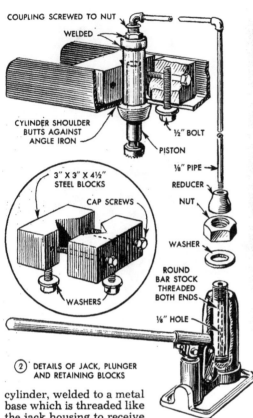

COUPLING SCREWED TO NUT

WELDED

CYLINDER SHOULDER
BUTTS AGAINST
ANGLE IRON

½" BOLT

PISTON

⅛" PIPE

3" X 3" X 4½"
STEEL BLOCKS

REDUCER

CAP SCREWS

NUT

WASHER

WASHERS

ROUND
BAR STOCK
THREADED
BOTH ENDS

⅛" HOLE

② DETAILS OF JACK, PLUNGER
AND RETAINING BLOCKS

cylinder, welded to a metal base which is threaded like the jack housing to receive the cylinder, and is drilled for the passage of fluid. A nut is welded to the base and a feed-pipe coupling screwed into it. The cylinder and piston in the substitute housing are mounted on the frame as shown in Fig. 2, upper detail, with the end of the housing resting on the angle iron and the shoulder of the cylinder butting up against the underside of the angle iron. The housing is clamped securely between the retaining blocks. In this position, the piston will press down on the work when fluid is pumped into the cylinder. The feed pipe is attached by couplings and elbows, and the jack is supported by a brace at the side of the frame. Coil springs, which are attached to the frame spacers by eyebolts, pull up the piston and force the fluid back when the valve is released.

Dressing Tool For Emery Wheel

The surface of an emery wheel can be dressed satisfactorily with a tool made from 10 steel washers and a 6-in. length of iron rod threaded at both ends to receive a nut. The washers are slipped over the rod and the nuts tightened to hold them fairly close together, but without preventing them

from rotating. The rod should be about ⅛ in. smaller than the diameter of the holes in the washers. In use, the tool is placed parallel with the surface to be dressed and held tightly against it while the wheel turns.

Holding Marking Die in Pipe Tee Prevents Injury to Workman

After repeated pounding with a hammer, the dies used in stamping numbers, initials, or other identifying marks on metal parts become rounded on top, permitting the hammer to strike a glancing blow which may hit the workman's fingers and so cause damage and loss of time. To avoid this threat of injury, one worker designed the die holder illustrated. It is made from two ⅜-in. pipe tees joined by a length of ⅜-in. pipe within which a ¼-in. pipe is inserted. With the die slipped in place, the tees are turned to tighten the inside pipe against it, thus holding it firmly.

⁋If you have occasion to use a drill that is too small to fit your brace, slip a piece of wire solder over the shank.

Hand-Powered
DRILL PRESS

By Arthur W. Howe

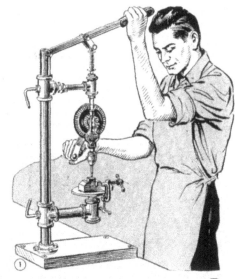

THERE'S no need to place work on the floor or climb up on the bench to put enough pressure on the drill if you have a hand-operated drill press. This particular one, Fig. 1, is made from a ½-in., 2-speed breast drill, although other sizes may be substituted. Either wood or metal is used for the base. The column is a 36-in. length of 1½-in. pipe. One end is threaded for a floor flange and the other end is notched for the operating lever. The pipe should be dressed so the two tees will be a smooth fit. These tees are reamed also and the backs are drilled and tapped for a ½-in. thread. Nuts are brazed in place in the following manner: thread them onto ½-in. bolts and turn the bolts into the tees until the nuts are flush against the tees. Then braze and remove the bolts. This will align the threads. Bend and thread short lengths of rod to make the adjusting screws.

The drill-press table is assembled as shown in Fig. 2. A short length of 1½-in. pipe is screwed to the tee on the column and an identical tee is fastened to the free end. A short nipple screws to this tee and connects to a floor flange and the table. For the upper assembly, bush the tee down for ¾-in. pipe. The nipple and tee here should center over the drill-press table. The upper left-hand detail shows how the ¾-in. tee is assembled with the ⅝-in. rod. If you have a drill with a removable handle, you may be able to insert the rod and lock it with a setscrew, or you may have to braze it to the drill. The lever is a length of flat iron with a wooden handle riveted on. A linkage connecting the lever to the rod is held with locked nuts and washers. Fig. 3 shows an easy way to make a foot-feed drill.

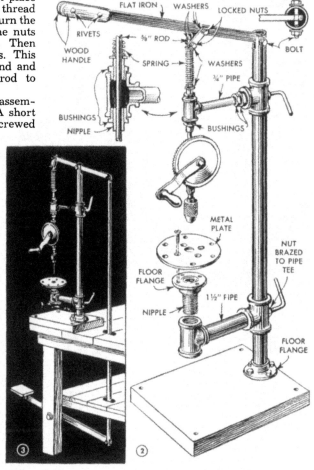

FLAT IRON WASHERS LOCKED NUTS
RIVETS ⅝" ROD BOLT
WOOD HANDLE SPRING WASHERS
¾" PIPE
BUSHINGS BUSHINGS
NIPPLE
METAL PLATE
NUT BRAZED TO PIPE TEE
FLOOR FLANGE
1½" PIPE
NIPPLE
FLOOR FLANGE

DRILL PRESS MADE FROM PIPE

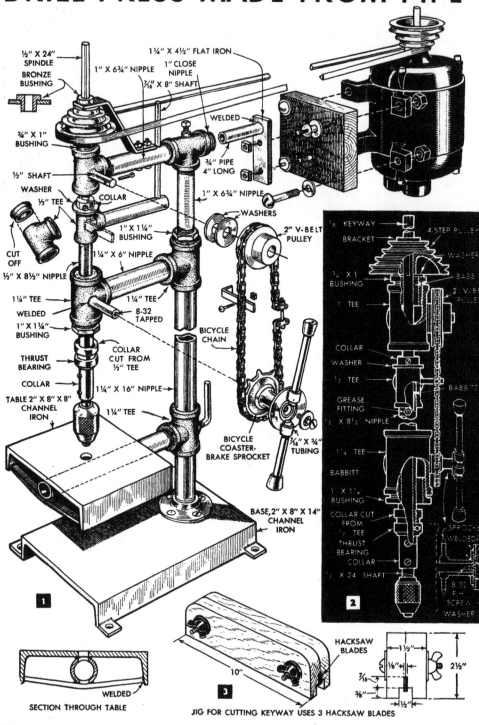

½" X 24" SPINDLE

BRONZE BUSHING

1¼" X 4½" FLAT IRON

1" X 6¾" NIPPLE

1" CLOSE NIPPLE

3/16" X 8" SHAFT

WELDED

¾" X 1" BUSHING

½" SHAFT

WASHER

½" TEE

COLLAR

CUT OFF

½" X 8½" NIPPLE

¾" PIPE 4" LONG

1" X 6¾" NIPPLE

WASHERS

1" X 1¼" BUSHING

2" V-BELT PULLEY

1¼" X 6" NIPPLE

1¼" TEE

WELDED

1" X 1¼" BUSHING

1¼" TEE

8-32 TAPPED

THRUST BEARING

COLLAR

TABLE 2" X 8" X 8" CHANNEL IRON

COLLAR CUT FROM ½" TEE

1¼" X 16" NIPPLE

1¼" TEE

BICYCLE CHAIN

BICYCLE COASTER-BRAKE SPROCKET

7/16" X ¾" TUBING

BASE, 2" X 8" X 14" CHANNEL IRON

KEYWAY

BRACKET

4-STEP PULLEY

WASHER

¾" X 1 BUSHING

BABBITT

2 V-BELT PULLEY

1 TEE

COLLAR

WASHER

½ TEE

GREASE FITTING

BABBITT

½ X 8½ NIPPLE

1¼ TEE

BABBITT

1 X 1¼ BUSHING

COLLAR CUT FROM ½ TEE

THRUST BEARING

COLLAR

½ X 24 SHAFT

SPROCKET

WELDED

8-32 F.H. SCREW

WASHER

1

2

HACKSAW BLADES

1½"

⅛"

7/16"

⅜"

2½"

½"

WELDED

SECTION THROUGH TABLE

10"

3

JIG FOR CUTTING KEYWAY USES 3 HACKSAW BLADES

FITTINGS

A practical tool for minimum outlay of time and money—that's the main feature of this 15-in. drill press made from pipe fittings

By James L. LeSuer

INEXPENSIVE and easy to assemble, this bench-type drill press is made mainly from pipe fittings. The hand-feed arrangement is simple and sensitive in action, giving a positive spindle feed which prevents breakage of small drills. Drill-press accessories driven by a ½-in. chuck, such as router bits, plug cutters, planer heads and disk sanders, can be used.

Fig. 1 details the assembly of the column and head and names the fittings used. First make the base, which is simply a piece of 8-in. channel iron cut to the length given, with four bolt lugs welded to the legs of the channel. While you are at it, make up the drill table also. For the column, use a 16-in. black-pipe nipple. This is easier to polish than galvanized pipe. Place the nipple in a vise and polish smooth with a strip of abrasive cloth. Grasp the abrasive strip at each end and loop it once about the pipe. Then pull alternately on the ends of the strip. Ream the 1¼-in. pipe tee, on which the table swivels, to an easy fit over the column. Drill a ⁵⁄₁₆-in. hole through the top of the tee and weld on a ⁵⁄₁₆-in. nut. Thread one end of a short length of ⁵⁄₁₆-in. rod, bend at right angles just above the thread and you have the locking screw to hold the table

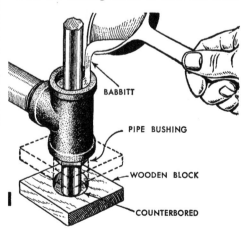

BABBITT

PIPE BUSHING

WOODEN BLOCK

COUNTERBORED

securely in any position on the column.

Build up the column and arms, beginning with a 1¼-in. floor flange attached to the base with four ⁵⁄₁₆-in. flatheaded cap screws, finishing this part of the assembly with all nipples, bushings, and all tees except those two which will form bearings for the spindle. Draw all joints tight. Weld ½-in. shafts to the bearing tees for the sprocket and idler pulley of the raising-and-lowering mechanism, Fig. 1. Then screw the tees onto the nipples and line them up. Fig. 2 details the spindle assembly. As indicated in Fig. 1 the spindle is 24 in. long and the first operation on it is cutting a ⅛-in. keyway extending from the top of the spindle to the bottom of the 4-step pulley, Fig. 2. Have this milled at the local machine shop or do it by hand with the improvised keyway cutter detailed in Fig. 3. Thread the lower end of the spindle to take the tapped mounting sleeve of a ½-in. chuck. By checking the spindle assembly in Figs. 1 and 2 you can see the sequence of operations necessary to put the parts together correctly. Because the supporting parts are made from pipe fittings, it is impossible to give precise dimensions for the location of bearings, collars and guides. This must be worked out by trial assembly. Fig. 4 shows how the babbitt bearings are poured, using a counterbored wooden block as a retainer.

Removable Speed-Reducing Unit for Drill Press

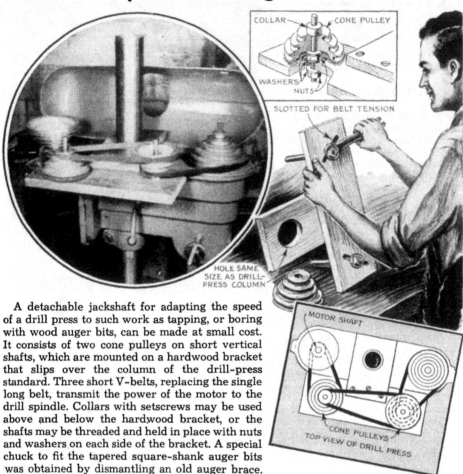

A detachable jackshaft for adapting the speed of a drill press to such work as tapping, or boring with wood auger bits, can be made at small cost. It consists of two cone pulleys on short vertical shafts, which are mounted on a hardwood bracket that slips over the column of the drill-press standard. Three short V-belts, replacing the single long belt, transmit the power of the motor to the drill spindle. Collars with setscrews may be used above and below the hardwood bracket, or the shafts may be threaded and held in place with nuts and washers on each side of the bracket. A special chuck to fit the tapered square-shank auger bits was obtained by dismantling an old auger brace.

Sheet-Metal Work Is Held Safely On Drill-Press Table

Small pieces of thin sheet metal can be held safely on a drill-press table with this simple clamp, which consists of a handle cut from ¾-in. stock and a bolt with washer and wing nut to fit. The underside of the handle is covered partially with a strip of fabric belting tacked or cemented in place while a hook is bent on the head end of the bolt so that it will slip over the table edge. In use, the work is placed under the wood strip and pressure is exerted on the handle to prevent the work from turning when operating the drill.

PRECISION DRILL·PRESS
for the modelmaker

By Alexander Maxwell

Table is elevated with hand control to feed work against drill held in stationary chuck

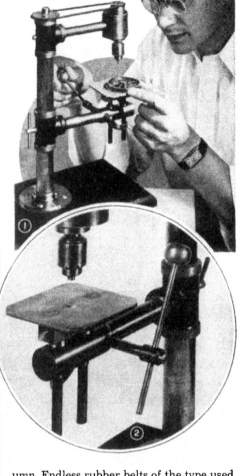

BY HAVING the table travel up and down instead of the chuck, the construction of the little drill press, shown in Fig. 1, is simplified to the point where all the parts can be machined completely on any small screw-cutting lathe. Standard stock materials are used—namely, the pipe fittings, bearings and chuck, while the rest of the parts are turned to size from odd

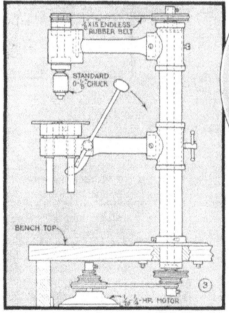

pieces of steel, brass and flat iron. Any small utility or sewing-machine motor will do to drive the press, although it is advisable to use a motor of the induction type having end thrust bearings, if it is to be mounted in a vertical position beneath the bench as shown. From Fig. 3 you can get a general idea of how the parts fit together, and how the chuck and motor are belted to a central jackshaft enclosed in the col-

umn. Endless rubber belts of the type used on vacuum cleaners provide a slip-free drive.

The column consists of a length of standard seamless-steel tubing at the lower end of which a pipe flange is held with setscrews as shown in the pull-apart view in Fig. 6, and in Fig. 10. The flange is chucked to the faceplate and the threads are bored out to make a wringing fit over the column. When turning cast iron, remember to take a deep initial cut to prevent the hard surface crust from taking the edge off your cutting tool.

Machining the pipe reducing tees to fit the column requires care. You will notice that one end of the upper tee is turned down to fit squarely in the shoulder cut

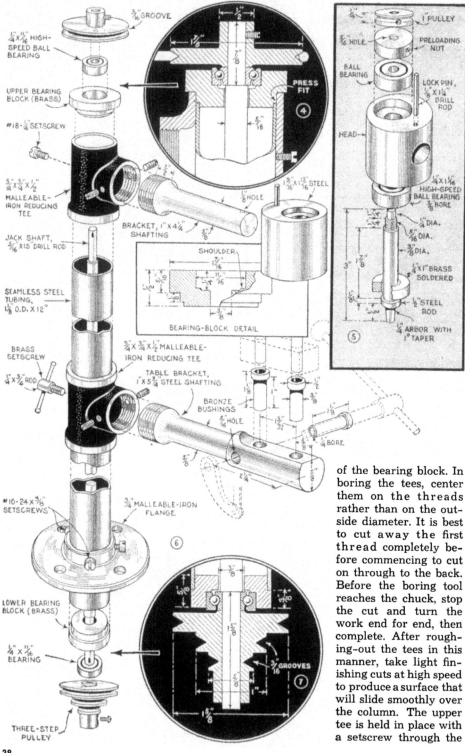

3/16" GROOVE

1/4"×1 1/16" HIGH-SPEED BALL BEARING

UPPER BEARING BLOCK (BRASS)

#18-1/4" SETSCREW

3/4"×3/4"×1/2" MALLEABLE-IRON REDUCING TEE

JACK SHAFT, 5/16"×15" DRILL ROD

SEAMLESS STEEL TUBING, 1 1/8" O.D.×12"

BRASS SETSCREW

1/4"×3/4" ROD

#10-24×3/8" SETSCREWS

3/4" MALLEABLE-IRON FLANGE

LOWER BEARING BLOCK (BRASS)

1/4"×1 1/16" BEARING

THREE-STEP PULLEY

BRACKET, 1"×4 1/4" SHAFTING

1/16" HOLE

PRESS FIT

④

5/16"

1/2"

1 3/8"

7/8"

5/16"

1 9/16"×1 3/16" STEEL

SHOULDER

1 7/16"

11/16"

3/8"

BEARING-BLOCK DETAIL

3/4"×3/4"×1/2" MALLEABLE-IRON REDUCING TEE

TABLE BRACKET, 1"×5 3/4" STEEL SHAFTING

BRONZE BUSHINGS

5/16" HOLE

1 3/32"

1/4" BORE

2 1/4"

⑥

1/8"

1"

1/2"

⑦

3/8"

1 5/8"

3/16" GROOVES

5/8"

1 5/8"

1/4" PULLEY

7/16" HOLE

BALL BEARING

HEAD

PRELOADING NUT

LOCK PIN, 1/8"×1 1/4" DRILL ROD

1/4"×1 1/16" HIGH-SPEED BALL BEARING 3/8" BORE

1/4" DIA.

5/16" DIA.

3/8" DIA.

1/4"×1" BRASS SOLDERED

1/2" STEEL ROD

3" 1 7/8"

1/4" ARBOR WITH 1° TAPER

⑤

of the bearing block. In boring the tees, center them on the threads rather than on the outside diameter. It is best to cut away the first thread completely before commencing to cut on through to the back. Before the boring tool reaches the chuck, stop the cut and turn the work end for end, then complete. After roughing-out the tees in this manner, take light finishing cuts at high speed to produce a surface that will slide smoothly over the column. The upper tee is held in place with a setscrew through the

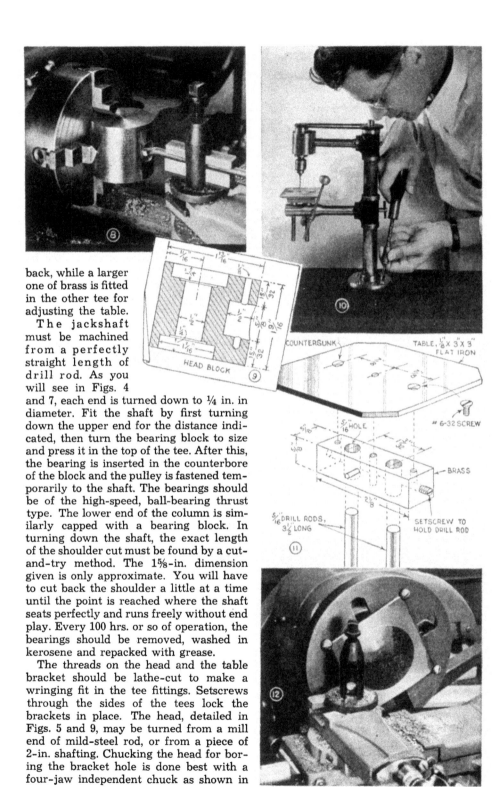

back, while a larger one of brass is fitted in the other tee for adjusting the table.

The jackshaft must be machined from a perfectly straight length of drill rod. As you will see in Figs. 4 and 7, each end is turned down to ¼ in. in diameter. Fit the shaft by first turning down the upper end for the distance indicated, then turn the bearing block to size and press it in the top of the tee. After this, the bearing is inserted in the counterbore of the block and the pulley is fastened temporarily to the shaft. The bearings should be of the high-speed, ball-bearing thrust type. The lower end of the column is similarly capped with a bearing block. In turning down the shaft, the exact length of the shoulder cut must be found by a cut-and-try method. The 1⅝-in. dimension given is only approximate. You will have to cut back the shoulder a little at a time until the point is reached where the shaft seats perfectly and runs freely without end play. Every 100 hrs. or so of operation, the bearings should be removed, washed in kerosene and repacked with grease.

The threads on the head and the table bracket should be lathe-cut to make a wringing fit in the tee fittings. Setscrews through the sides of the tees lock the brackets in place. The head, detailed in Figs. 5 and 9, may be turned from a mill end of mild-steel rod, or from a piece of 2-in. shafting. Chucking the head for boring the bracket hole is done best with a four-jaw independent chuck as shown in

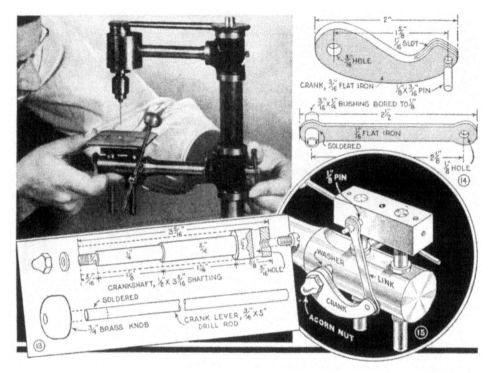

CRANK, 3/16" FLAT IRON   1/8" X 3/16" PIN

3/16" X 1/4" BUSHING BORED TO 1/8"

1/16" FLAT IRON
SOLDERED

14

CRANKSHAFT, 1/2 X 3 3/16" SHAFTING
SOLDERED
3/4" BRASS KNOB   CRANK LEVER, 3/16" X 5"
DRILL ROD
13

1/8" PIN

WASHER   LINK

CRANK

ACORN NUT   15

Fig. 8. Start the hole with a drill and then use a boring tool to cut a force-fit hole for the bracket. A rawhide mallet is used to drive the two together, after which they are pinned. When properly bored and counterbored to receive the bearings and the spindle, the head should look like the sectional view in Fig. 9. The 1-deg. taper on the lower end of the spindle must be cut accurately to seat the drill chuck perfectly.

The chuck, which should be of the high-speed balanced type, is pressed on the spindle by hand. The preloading nut is screwed down to provide constant pressure on the bearings. Tighten it until the bearings bind, then loosen it slowly until they will just turn freely.

If your lathe is large enough to swing the table bracket, drill the holes for the bronze sleeve bushings with a drill held in the tailstock chuck. The front bushing is a press fit in the bracket, while the other one can be left slightly loose to compensate for any slight offset in drilling. Fig. 12 shows how the table may be held at the corners with screws and surfaced, both sides, on the faceplate. The best way to register the holes in the carriage with those in the bracket is to bore one hole first and insert the rod. Then with one end of the

other rod pointed slightly, pass it through the bushing and center-punch the under-side of the carriage. The parts for the table-raising mechanism are detailed in Figs. 6, 13 and 14, while Figs. 2 and 15 show how they will look when assembled. The drill-rod washer should bear against the shoulder of the crankshaft and not the end of the bushing, so that the acorn nut when tightened will hold the crank in place.

Pattern Is Fastened to Plastic With Rubber Cement

PAPER
GLUED TO
BAKELITE

Instead of scratching a design in the surface of hard plastics like Bakelite for a guide in cutting, glue paper over the work, using rubber cement, and sketch the design or pattern on it. Then, if necessary, a correction can be made in the design without marring the surface of the work. The paper can be removed without any trouble after the cutting or drilling has been done.

From SEWING MACHINE to JIGSAW

By GUST M. LARSON

THAT old sewing machine long relegated to the attic can be converted into an excellent motor-driven jigsaw at practically no cost. All you have to do is strip the machine of its shuttle mechanism, located on the underside of the base, and install the blade-tension device shown at the right. Thickness of the stock that the saw will handle depends upon the stroke of the machine at hand, although it is possible to increase the stroke of most machines simply by raising the needle bar in the head. Drive is by a ½ or ⅓-hp. motor mounted on a hinged base to bring it in line with the pulley on the handwheel. A small insect sprayer, attached by brackets to the cover plate, is operated by the needle bar to provide an efficient sawdust blower.

The machine can be left on its original stand, or you can set the head and base flush in the top of a sturdy bench. In either case, a board must be installed, as shown in the cutaway view, so that the tensioner can be screwed to it, directly below and in line with the needle bar. The tension device consists of a floor flange threaded to a slotted tube in which slides a spring-loaded shaft. The tension of the spring is adjusted by a nut at the end to suit the blade being used. A cross pin keeps the shaft from turning in the tube, and a collar and setscrew, soldered to the upper end of the shaft, form a blade clamp. The needle clamp will hold jeweler's blades but will require enlarging for saber-type blades.

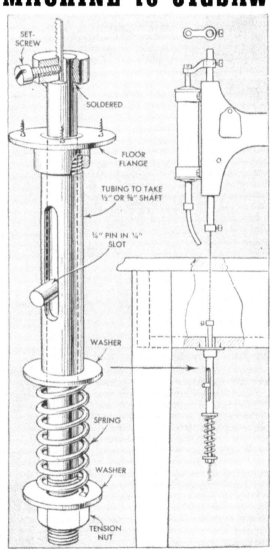

SET-SCREW

SOLDERED

FLOOR FLANGE

TUBING TO TAKE ½" OR ⅝" SHAFT

¼" PIN IN ¼" SLOT

WASHER

SPRING

WASHER

TENSION NUT

Bushing Puller Makes Gear Changing Easy

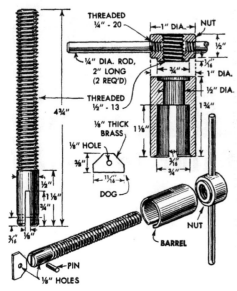

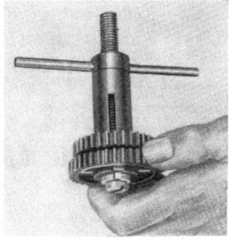

.By altering dimensions, this bushing puller can be made up for a wide range of sizes. It gives a straight pull that does not damage the work

On some change-gear lathes it is necessary to pull the bushings of individual gears when making setups for various carriage speeds and for thread cutting. To speed up this job and also to avoid any danger of damaging the parts, make the handy bushing puller, detailed above. It is dimensioned for lathe-gear bushings having a ¾-in. outside diameter and a ½-in. bore. By altering dimensions of the barrel and the threaded puller rod, the tool can be made to fit bushings of other sizes and types. The barrel is turned from cold-rolled steel. The rod must be slightly smaller in diameter than the bore of the bushing and the barrel must be bored slightly larger than the outside diameter of the bushing. Slots in the barrel allow keys on the lathe-gear bushings to pass, but for straight sleeve bushings the slots are not needed. The rod is turned from ½-in. steel shafting and threaded with a ½-13 thread. The unthreaded end is slotted to receive a brass dog pivoted on a pin to allow it to pass through the bushing. Brass or bronze is used for the nut, which is turned with a ¹⁄₁₆-in. shoulder to seat in a counterbore as shown. To use the puller, the nut is turned back on the rod, and the rod, with the dog in the folded position, is passed through the bushing. Then turn the dog to engage the end of the bushing.

Index Mark on Compound Slide Shows Maximum Cross-Feed Limits

Accidentally backing a compound slide off the feed screw on a metal-turning lathe will not happen if a white index mark is painted on the saddle and the bottom slide of the rest to show the operator the maximum length of the thread. Run the cross-feed out to the limits of the thread before marking. This makes it easy to prevent running out the saddle too far by merely watching the marks and stopping when the two are aligned. This idea is especially helpful when a beginner is unfamiliar with the compound slide. If you wish, the index marks can be made by applying narrow strips of adhesive tape instead of paint to the saddle and bottom slide.

BENDING BRAKES
for Your Sheet-Metal Jobs

By Sam Brown

THESE bending brakes will simplify sheet-metal fabrication. Two designs are described, both capable of bending 24-ga. galvanized iron the width of the brake, or heavier metal when the bend is not at full 12-in. capacity. Design No. 2, Fig. 8, while more difficult to make, is somewhat superior in that it offers stronger construction and also permits partial (tab) and reverse bends which are not possible with No. 1 design.

Design No. 1: Both designs are of the folding-leaf variety, and the general features of construction are grasped easily from Fig. 3. The essential feature is that the center of hinge pin must line up exactly with the meeting edges of folding leaf and table. This is diagramed in Fig. 4. The working of the brake is shown in Fig. 1, the metal being clamped under the forming bar and then bent by pulling up on the folding leaf. The forming bar should be notched for easy removal. It is positioned exactly for duplicate work by means of two sliding

BENDING METAL TILE—ONE OF MANY JOBS POSSIBLE WITH BRAKE

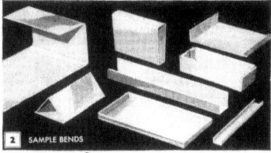

2 SAMPLE BENDS

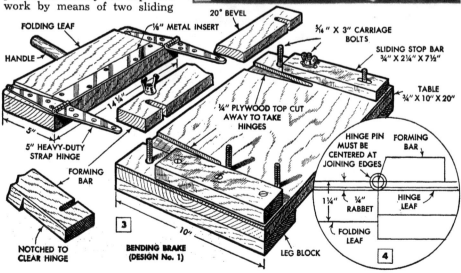

FOLDING LEAF

HANDLE

20° BEVEL

⅛" METAL INSERT

⁵⁄₁₆" X 3" CARRIAGE BOLTS

SLIDING STOP BAR ¾" X 2¼" X 7½"

TABLE ¾" X 10" X 20"

14¼"

¼" PLYWOOD TOP CUT AWAY TO TAKE HINGES

5"

5" HEAVY-DUTY STRAP HINGE

FORMING BAR

NOTCHED TO CLEAR HINGE

3

10"

BENDING BRAKE (DESIGN No. 1)

LEG BLOCK

HINGE PIN MUST BE CENTERED AT JOINING EDGES

FORMING BAR

1¼" ¼" RABBET

HINGE LEAF

FOLDING LEAF

4

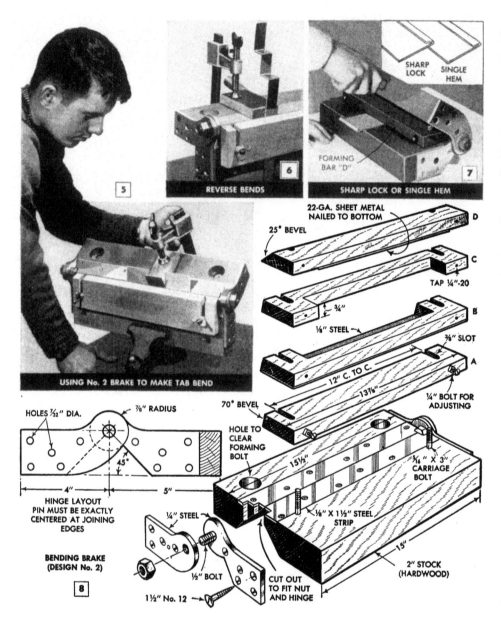

5

6 REVERSE BENDS

SHARP LOCK SINGLE HEM

7 SHARP LOCK OR SINGLE HEM

FORMING BAR "D"

USING No. 2 BRAKE TO MAKE TAB BEND

22-GA. SHEET METAL NAILED TO BOTTOM

D

25° BEVEL

C

TAP ¼"-20

¾"

⅛" STEEL

B

⅜" SLOT

12" C. TO C.

13⅞"

A

¼" BOLT FOR ADJUSTING

HOLES ⁷⁄₃₂" DIA.

⅞" RADIUS

45°

4"

5"

HINGE LAYOUT
PIN MUST BE EXACTLY
CENTERED AT JOINING
EDGES

BENDING BRAKE
(DESIGN No. 2)

8

70° BEVEL

HOLE TO
CLEAR
FORMING
BOLT

15½"

⅛" X 1½" STEEL
STRIP

¼" STEEL

½" BOLT

1½" No. 12

CUT OUT
TO FIT NUT
AND HINGE

⁵⁄₁₆" X 3"
CARRIAGE
BOLT

15"

2" STOCK
(HARDWOOD)

stop bars, as can be seen in Fig. 3. One of these works along a fixed block to provide a guide for right-angle bends. Any kind of wood can be used for folding leaf and table, but the forming bar must be hardwood or softwood faced with metal. The hinge should not be lighter than specified and is better made a little heavier.

Design No. 2: This is shown in Fig. 8. It is a heavier and more compact design than No. 1, and requires special hinges cut from ¼-in. steel, as shown. The 45-deg. cut on the underside of leaf and table weakens the construction somewhat, but offers an arrangement that is essential for reverse bends. The four styles of forming bars shown in Fig. 8 will handle all ordinary work. Care should be taken in assembly to get the pivot points in perfect alignment. This design also will work out nicely with hinges made from ¾-in. plywood, pinning the bolt to the table member and providing a brass bushing in

44

the other member to prevent excessive wear and loose action.

Tab and reverse bends: Tab and reverse bends are worked on No. 2 brake by mounting the brake on edge in a vise and folding the leaf all the way back. A block of wood is clamped to the folding leaf and becomes the forming member. Fig. 5 shows the operation on a tab bend; Fig. 6 shows the same setup for reverse bends. Neither can be done on the No. 1 brake.

Standard operations: The sharp lock, Fig. 7, is made by using the brake in a normal position with a style-D forming bar. This bend is used frequently for fastening two pieces of metal together. If the bend is at full capacity (12 in. long), it is best to form it to a flange with the stronger A or B bar and then complete the lock with the sharp-edge D bar. The single sharp lock when pressed tightly together in a vise or by hammering becomes the single hem or bend, as shown. If the single bend is hemmed again, it makes a double hem. At full capacity on a narrow hem less than

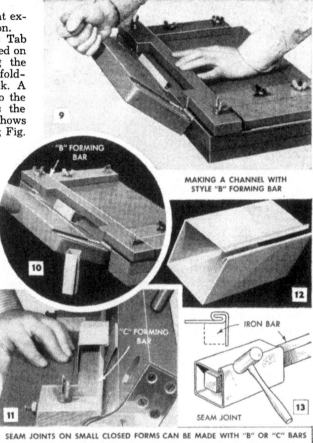

MAKING A CHANNEL WITH STYLE "B" FORMING BAR

"B" FORMING BAR

"C" FORMING BAR

IRON BAR

SEAM JOINT

SEAM JOINTS ON SMALL CLOSED FORMS CAN BE MADE WITH "B" OR "C" BARS

¼ in. wide, this bend offers the ultimate strength and accuracy test for your brake —a poorly made brake will fail in this double-hem operation.

Large return bends or channels are made with the standard forming bar (style A), and offer no difficulties. Smaller channels are made with the B bar, which permits working as small as ⅛-in. cross section. This operation is shown in Fig. 9. The B bar is used also for bending small closed forms, as shown in Fig. 10. As can be seen, the brake does not fully close the form on the final bend, but it is close enough so that a little springing by hand will complete it. Style-C bar offers another way of working small closed forms, as shown in Fig. 11. Complete closure is possible with

this bar, but the work must be resprung to remove it from the bar. When the closed form has a seam joint, Fig. 12, the final bend, as in Fig. 11, is really a reverse bend and is best worked by the method shown in Fig. 5. However, the reverse caused by the narrow flange is slight and does not materially affect the bending operation. Fig. 13 shows how the seam joint is closed by hammering. This is not an easy joint to make and should be practiced before you attempt it on finished work.

Box bends: One of the most used forms of sheet-metal work is the simple square box. Like its companion in wood, it can be made a dozen different ways. Simplest way is to cut out the corners and then bend the work over a forming block, Fig. 14, or over

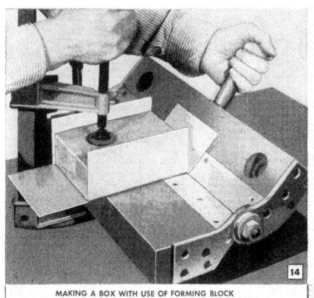

flange which can be riveted or soldered to the sides (a sample is shown in Fig. 2), and this style is made easily by first forming the tabs, working as shown in Fig. 5, and then bending the sides over a forming block.

Work capacity: Work capacity of both brakes described is about 12 in. No. 2 design will work satisfactorily up to about 18-24 in. No. 1 brake will not handle metal thicker than 24 ga. (usual furnace-pipe weight as obtained at tin shops); No. 2 brake will work 22-ga. material. Both will handle much thicker metal if the bend is short. Dimensions given are working specifications and can be varied.

MAKING A BOX WITH USE OF FORMING BLOCK

a special style-A forming bar, Fig. 15. For the latter operation, the forming bar has notches cut to accommodate the flanges previously turned up. The notches (saw kerfs) do not affect the bend, and one bar can be notched many times to suit different sizes of work. The simple style of box shown, while easy to bend, presents a fair amount of work in soldering the corners. Some shapes in this style (such as lids), if shallow, are often strong enough not to require soldering. Most larger boxes make use of some kind of inside or outside

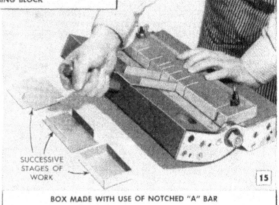

BOX MADE WITH USE OF NOTCHED "A" BAR

Slots Cut Through Steel Plate Aid in Bending It

A piece of ¼-in. steel plate can be bent in a vise with comparative ease and without the usual equipment, if it is first slotted along the bend line with a torch. Leave about 1¼ in. of material between the slots and at the ends. Should it be necessary to strengthen the plate after bending, fill the channels formed by the slots with welding rod.

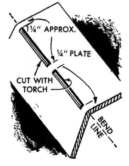

Adjustable Wooden Hold-Down

To hold work flat while being surfaced with a drill-press shaping tool, an adjustable wooden hold-down bolted to the fence will assure smooth, even cutting with no danger of gouging the work. The hold-down, which is made from a length of 2 by 4-in. stock or similar material, is recessed in the center to fit around the cutterhead, and near each end for bolts inserted through slots that allow adjustment of the hold-down. The lower edge is rubbed with paraffin to permit work to slide freely.

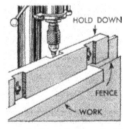

Motorized HAND PLANE
gives smooth finish

JUST the thing for edging long boards, fitting doors and jointing smaller pieces of stock at the bench, this electric hand plane is made from a discarded vacuum-cleaner motor, a piece of hardwood, some sheet aluminum and a few small bolts. If you've ever had the rather disagreeable task of fitting a door with the ordinary hand plane you will appreciate this tool, as the high-speed cutter whisks away the waste wood down to the dimension line in a fraction of the time and besides, it leaves a glass-smooth surface. Or, if you need a jointer just turn the machine upside down and clamp the handle in the bench vise as in Fig. 4. In this position

it's especially handy for squaring up small pieces of stock.

Figs. 1, 2 and 3 tell practically the whole story of the assembly. Of course, the arrangement of the parts shown is that suited to the characteristics of one particular motor. This means that if another motor of somewhat different design is used, minor

changes in details of the assembly may be necessary. Now referring to Figs. 5 to 8 inclusive, you'll get a good idea of how the parts are made. The guide, Fig. 5, is bolted to the motor and then to the base, Fig. 7. A slotted bolt hole, Fig. 5, provides a means of adjusting the depth of cut. You will notice from Figs. 1 and 3 that the fan housing has been cut and fitted to the plane in such a way that it forms a combination knife guard and dust chute. The fan housings of most vacuum cleaners can be adapted in the manner shown by a bit of careful work with the hacksaw and a file.

The cutterhead is shown in Fig. 8. It is of the square two-knife type and is drilled to fit over the motor shaft. Perfect running balance is of the utmost importance as the head must operate without vibration at high speed. This means that the hole for the motor shaft has to be exactly centered and the cutting edges of the knives must describe the same arc. One way to test the head for static balance is to mount it on a short length of shafting with the ends projecting equally. Then fasten

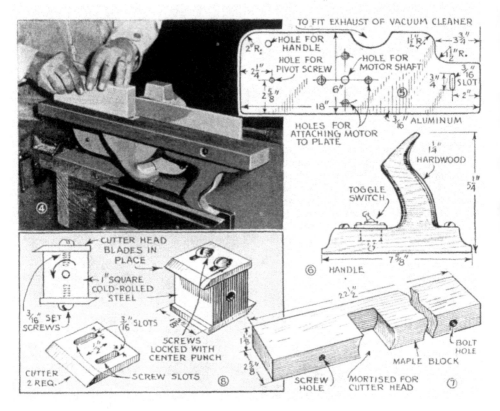

two razor blades to a block of wood, level them, and place the head with the ends of the shaft resting on the edges of the blades. If the head is even slightly heavy on one side it will immediately roll until this side is down. To correct this tendency you remove metal on the heavy side of the head with a file until the head will roll on the razor-blade edges without coming to rest at any one point.

Hints on Protecting Tools and Instruments From Rust

Fused calcium chloride can be used to prevent tools and instruments from rusting if they are stored in airtight cans or containers. A few lumps of calcium chloride are placed in a wide-mouth, uncorked glass bottle, which is then set in the can with the tools. The calcium chloride rapidly absorbs moisture from the air. After some months of use, the chemical will have collected so much moisture from the air that it has changed to a liquid. It should then be replaced, or renewed by heating it until the water has evaporated. Fine instruments, such as balances and micrometers, that have become rusted may be cleaned by rubbing them with a soft cloth moistened with a rust solvent, which is made by mixing equal parts of oleic acid, ammonia, and denatured alcohol. After mixing, this solution should be filtered through cloth to remove any particles of foreign matter that might scratch the work being cleaned. When the rust has been removed, the instruments should be polished with precipitated chalk, which is applied with a soft cloth moistened in fine oil. Tools that cannot be stored in a dry place may be protected from rust by coating them with a paste made by melting together lard, 8 oz., and pure rosin, 1 oz. When cool, add enough benzine to make a paste. This should be applied in a thin, even layer with a fine cloth.

How To Make a . . .

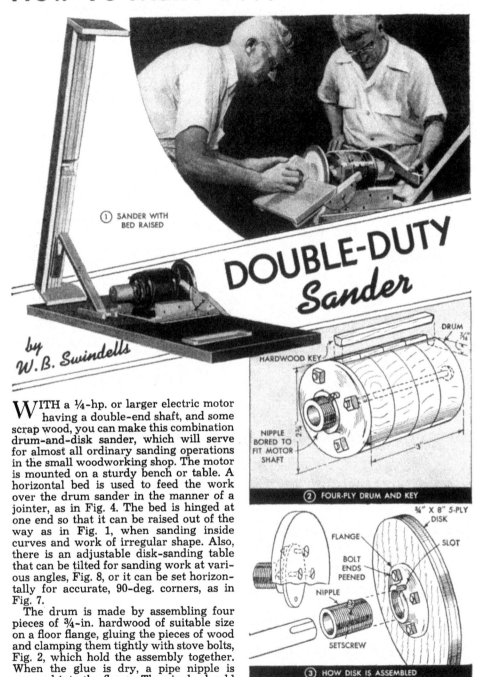

(1) SANDER WITH BED RAISED

DOUBLE-DUTY
Sander

by W. B. Swindells

HARDWOOD KEY

DRUM ¾" ¾"

NIPPLE BORED TO FIT MOTOR SHAFT

2¾"

3"

(2) FOUR-PLY DRUM AND KEY

FLANGE

¾" X 8" 5-PLY DISK

SLOT

BOLT ENDS PEENED

NIPPLE

SETSCREW

(3) HOW DISK IS ASSEMBLED

WITH a ¼-hp. or larger electric motor having a double-end shaft, and some scrap wood, you can make this combination drum-and-disk sander, which will serve for almost all ordinary sanding operations in the small woodworking shop. The motor is mounted on a sturdy bench or table. A horizontal bed is used to feed the work over the drum sander in the manner of a jointer, as in Fig. 4. The bed is hinged at one end so that it can be raised out of the way as in Fig. 1, when sanding inside curves and work of irregular shape. Also, there is an adjustable disk-sanding table that can be tilted for sanding work at various angles, Fig. 8, or it can be set horizontally for accurate, 90-deg. corners, as in Fig. 7.

The drum is made by assembling four pieces of ¾-in. hardwood of suitable size on a floor flange, gluing the pieces of wood and clamping them tightly with stove bolts, Fig. 2, which hold the assembly together. When the glue is dry, a pipe nipple is screwed into the flange. The nipple should wood and flange are turned to a diameter of 2¾ in. Then the work is removed and a slot is cut lengthwise for a hardwood key that holds sheets of abrasive paper tightly around the drum.

Fig. 3 shows the sanding disk, which is a piece of plywood of the kind used in concrete forms. This is waterproof and will not warp. It is mounted on a floor flange and sleeve in the same manner as the drum, except that in this case the bolt heads must be countersunk in the face of the disk.

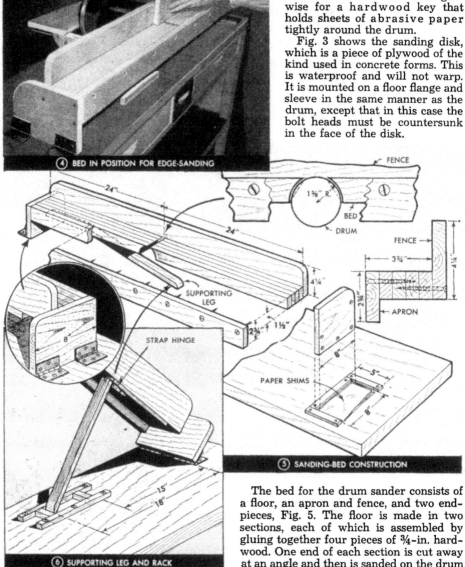

④ BED IN POSITION FOR EDGE-SANDING

⑤ SANDING-BED CONSTRUCTION

⑥ SUPPORTING LEG AND RACK

fit on the motor shaft snugly and reaming may be necessary. Or you can make up a sleeve from solid stock, drilling it to shaft size and threading one end to fit the flange. Then the nipple is drilled and tapped and the flange is slotted as shown to take a setscrew that locks the nipple and flange to the motor shaft. Now, the assembly is mounted in a lathe with a faceplate and dog, so that the center line through the nipple is in line with the lathe center. Both

The bed for the drum sander consists of a floor, an apron and fence, and two endpieces, Fig. 5. The floor is made in two sections, each of which is assembled by gluing together four pieces of ¾-in. hardwood. One end of each section is cut away at an angle and then is sanded on the drum so that when the sections are assembled there will be a concave cutout of 1⅜-in. radius over the drum as shown in the upper detail of Fig. 5. The apron and fence are screwed to the floor sections as in the right-hand detail, the screws also serving to supplement the glue in holding the floor strips together. The floor of the bed must be flush with the top of the drum without a covering of abrasive paper. Next, the endpieces of the bed are screwed in place, with their upper edge flush with the bed floor. One of the endpieces is hinged to the work table; the other is held in a stabilizing frame consisting of three cleats. Paper shims are placed in the frame to regulate the height of the bed above the drum to accommodate varying thicknesses of abrasive and to permit sanding work to desired depths. When the bed is raised, it is supported by a leg set in a rack as in Fig. 6.

The disk-sanding unit, consisting of table and base, is shown in Fig. 9. The base can be made of ¾-in. plywood or other suitable stock, cut in the form of the letter H, so that the motor base will

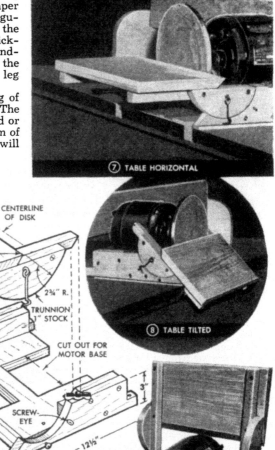

7 TABLE HORIZONTAL

8 TABLE TILTED

1" X 7" X 14"

CENTERLINE OF DISK

¼"

1/16" CLEARANCE

TILTING TABLE

TURN BUTTON

SEAT FOR CLEAT

2¾" R.

TRUNNION 1" STOCK

¾" PLYWOOD BASE

CUT OUT FOR MOTOR BASE

SCREW-EYE

3"

5"

14"

12½"

9 ASSEMBLY OF TABLE AND BASE

fit into the rear cutout and the edge of the disk can turn freely in the other. Sides are added to the base as supports for trunnions, on which the table rides. The trunnions are screwed to cleats attached to the underside of the table as shown. Each trunnion is half of a 5½-in. disk less the thickness of the table. The upper surface of the table, when horizontal, should be ¾ in. below the center of the sanding disk, and there should be a clearance of 1/16 in. between the table edge and the sanding disk when abrasive paper is attached. With the table in the horizontal position, the cleats rest on supporting pieces screwed to the sides of the base, and are held by turn buttons. A screen-door hook on each trunnion is slipped over screws driven part way into the sides. These also help to hold the table firmly in the horizontal position. To hold

the table in a 45-deg. position, as in Fig. 8, the hooks engage screw eyes located in the base. Screws and screw eyes should be positioned so that considerable pressure is required to release the hooks in order to prevent play, which otherwise may be considerable.

With a drum and disk of the sizes given here, you can use one 9 by 11-in. sheet of abrasive to cover both; an 8-in. disk and a 3 by 9-in. piece to fit the drum, leaving a 1 by 8-in. strip.

Improvised TOOL-POST GRINDER

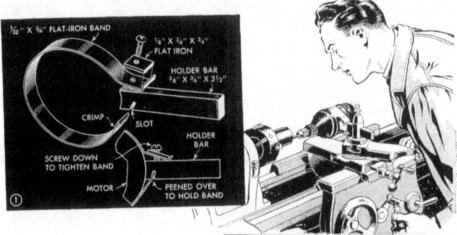

WHERE surface smoothness is more important than accuracy on small parts, high-speed grinding is often the answer. Most small grinders of the type ordinarily held in the hand are equipped either with a conventional drill chuck or with a collet-type chuck and make excellent tool-post grinders when fitted into a suitable holder. Many of these tiny motors are designed for speeds up to 20,000 r.p.m., which makes them especially suited to light grinding operations where a mirror finish on round work is the thing. A holder is made as detailed in Fig. 1, the trick being to get the compression band just the right length.

An example of work on which these improvised grinders do a first-class job is making a mandrel, Fig. 2. Select a length of steel rod and turn it until the working diameter is .001 in. greater than the hole it is to fit. Set the compound rest to about .5 deg., Fig. 2, and feed the grinder along the work cutting a taper of about .01 in. per foot. Make another pass of the grinding wheel at the same carriage setting and then lap the surface of the work with a hard slipstone and oil. On a mandrel, smoothness is more important than hardness, but if it is to be used for production runs, caseharden the center bearing surfaces of both ends. The mandrel can be pressed in and out of the work with an arbor press and being highly polished it will not freeze in the work.

Slicing glass tubing into spacer rings, Fig. 3, is a simple and rapid operation. An abrasive disk scores the glass and the heat snaps it off. Certain types of glass are a bit more involved. A diamond disk is used and the tube is cut all the way through.

Glass-smooth finish on a lathe mandrel is possible with a small high-speed grinder set up like this. Speeds up to 20,000 r.p.m. are common

Spacers are cut from glass tubing in a jiffy with this setup. The wheel scores the glass and a brush dipped in ice water snaps off the ring

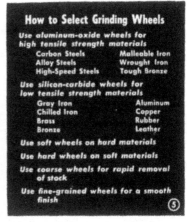

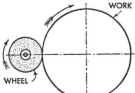

FOR EXTERNAL GRINDING, WHEEL ROTATES IN SAME DIRECTION AS THE WORK

FOR INTERNAL GRINDING, WHEEL ROTATES IN DIRECTION OPPOSITE THAT OF THE WORK

Diamond disks must run in thick soapsuds. If the tube resists breaking, touch it with a brush dipped in ice water.

Seamless tubing seldom is truly circular, but it can easily be trued up by dressing lightly with the wheel as in Fig. 4. For much of this work it is important to select a wheel that cuts without clogging or heating unduly, Fig. 5. Shellac-bonded wheels are generally used, but fine rubber wheels will do almost as well. The diamond disk is a wafer of soft iron or copper in which diamond dust has been embedded.

Work is rotated in the direction opposite to wheel travel for internal grinding, Fig. 6. Correct cutting speed is about 5000 surface ft. per min. with most wheels. Hence speed of the grinder should be about 15,200 r.p.m. with a 1-in. wheel. As most grinders turn 20,000 r.p.m. they are designed to run with a smaller wheel on stationary work. When the work rotates, Fig. 6, an allowance must be made. Small wheels require faster work rotation and large wheels slower. Before using a large wheel in a constant-speed grinder, check with the wheel speed recommended by the manufacturer.

Inexpensive Miter Box of Wood Has Pivoted Saw Guide

With this homemade miter box, the saw is swung either left or right to get the different angles. The base of the box is made of 1½-in. stock and the back is made of 1¼-in. wood. A ¾-in. dowel notched to take the saw is pivoted into a hole at the back. The notch should be of a depth to permit the saw teeth to just barely touch the base. Holes are drilled near the front edge of the base at various angles from the notched dowel to take a ½-in. dowel, which serves as a stop for the side of the saw. In use, the stop is set in the hole representing the angle at which the work is to be cut and the saw is placed in the notched pivot pin, after which the saw is held against the stop while making the cut.

¶Punches and chisels for modelmakers can be had by grinding ice picks to shape.

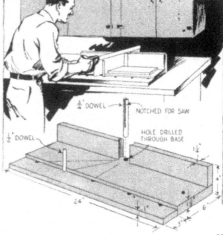

¾" DOWEL — NOTCHED FOR SAW

½" DOWEL

HOLE DRILLED THROUGH BASE

Ball-Bearing Mandrel From Bicycle Pedal Hanger

With very little alteration, a pedal-hanger assembly provides a rugged, inexpensive ball-bearing mandrel for a homemade power grinder, circular saw and similar high-speed tools

If you are planning a homemade tool that requires the use of a mandrel, such as a grinder, table saw, etc., the pedal-bearing assembly of a discarded bicycle will provide a ball-bearing mandrel that is free running and dust tight. Saw the frame to sever the hanger and weld the remaining stubs to a metal plate to simplify mounting the assembly. Then remove the pedal cranks and turn down the projecting ends of the shaft to the desired diameter; usually a ½-in. diameter is the most suitable. Threading the turned ends of the shaft so that nuts can be driven on in the direction opposite that of the saw or grinder rotation completes the job. If desired, a grease fitting can be fitted on the housing to simplify lubricating the bearings.

Drill for Modelmakers Assembled From Scrap Parts

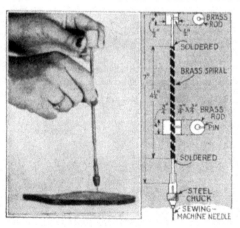

This handy drill for use in making model ships, planes, etc., is constructed easily. A 7-in. length of ⅛-in. brass or steel rod is used for the shaft, and a spiral, removed from an automatic lead pencil, serves as a rotating device, which is soldered at the ends to the brass shaft. A finger grip, which rotates the drill when moved up and down the spiral, is made from a ¾-in. length of brass rod. This has a hole drilled through the center so it will slide loosely over the spiral, and is fitted with a pin, which extends slightly into the center of the hole to engage the spiral. The chuck is one removed from a small pin drill. Drill bits are made from steel sewing-machine needles.

12-INCH DISK SANDER

has tilting table

By Paul F. Sass, Jr.

SQUARING UP small, rough-sawed parts, smoothing end grain and finishing the edges on plywood—these are quick, easy jobs for a disk sander, and at the same time are among the most difficult and tedious to do by hand. Exclusive of the motor, which can be ¼ to ½-hp., 1725-r.p.m. capacity, the sander is made from odds and ends that are found around most workshops, and only hand tools are needed for its construction.

Dimensions for the motor-mounting block are omitted because they will vary with the motor that is used. As far as height is concerned, the center line of the motor should be 1 in. above the tilt-table top, or 6½ in. above the base and, lengthwise of course, it centers on the base. Bolt the motor to the block and countersink holes for the nuts and washers, Fig. 1. The base is slotted to provide for adjustment of the motor, and these slots are countersunk also, Fig. 3, so the block mounting nuts and washers can be recessed. Make the slots a little wider than the diameter of the bolts to provide adjustment sideways. The table and tilt top are screwed to a pipe-and-flange pedestal that is 3½ in. from the end of the base opposite the motor. Dimensions for

Sanding surfaces at any desired angle is not difficult because the tilting table is adjustable

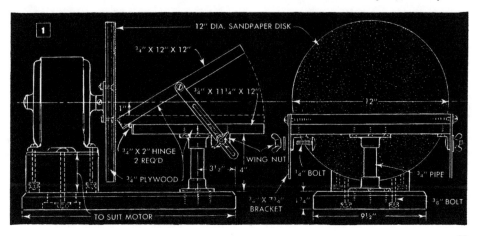

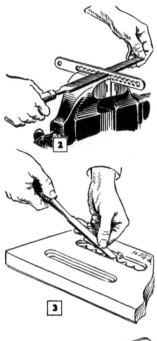

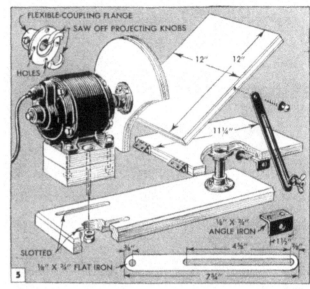

the table and tilt top, which are ¾-in. plywood, are given in Fig. 5, as are the details of the adjusting brackets. The slots for the brackets are drilled and filed as indicated in Fig. 2. Two butt hinges are used to secure the tilt top to the table, allowing the former to overlap the latter as shown in the left-hand detail of Fig. 1. A flexible-coupling flange is used as a mounting for the sanding disk. The face is cut off flush with a hacksaw, Fig. 4; or, to insure a disk that will run true, it can be faced in a lathe if the latter is available. To complete the sander, cut a ¾-in.-plywood disk 12 in. in diameter and bolt it to the flange with flat-head screws, countersinking the holes so the heads will be a little below the surface of the disk. Glue on the sand-paper and finish the unit with gray or black paint. For convenience in operation, a toggle switch can be mounted on the base or block to control the operation of the motor instead of using a switch in the line or on the wall.

Heats to Temper Homemade Tools Checked With Solder

The home mechanic who makes up small tools from drill rod or similar steel, will find that the following methods of gauging tempering heats and hardening the metals produce very accurate results. Instead of quenching the metal in water, heavy machine oil or boiled linseed oil is used, the tool being heated to a very bright cherry red, but below a white, sparkling heat. This is necessary as the oil quenches slower than water, giving the required hardness and increasing the strength and toughness. After this preliminary hardening, the tool is polished for some distance back of the working edge. Then it is heated slowly by applying a blowtorch flame about 1 in. back of the working edge until the metal just

begins to change color, after which it is tested by touching a piece of half-and-half solid wire solder to the heated portion. If the solder melts instantly, remove the tool, and as the heat works toward the edge, keep testing with the solder. When this barely melts when pressed firmly on the edge, quench the tool in water instantly and it will be of the right hardness for working in wood, leather and soft metals. For punches, cold chisels, etc., the metal should be just hot enough to melt the solder after a couple of light rubbing strokes.

⟨To free metal articles of rust, dip them in pure cider vinegar, leave it on for a few days, then rinse and dry thoroughly.

DRILL-PRESS

CIRCLE CUTTERS

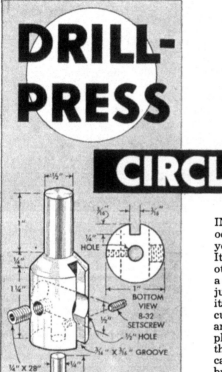

1 BOTTOM VIEW
8-32 SETSCREW
½" HOLE
¾" X ³⁄₁₆" GROOVE
¼" HOLE
1"
¼"
1¼"
¼" X 28" SETSCREW
GUIDE PIN

2 GROUND FLAT
CUTTING-BIT ARM
½" DIA.
8-32 SET-SCREW
CUTTING TOOLS
RESULTING EDGE OF CUT MATERIAL
LATHE TOOL BIT

IN THE AVERAGE JOB SHOP there's only occasional need for a circle cutter, but when you do need one you generally need it badly. It does work which is impractical to do by any other means except in a lathe or perhaps with a hole saw, that is, if you happen to have one just the right size for the work at hand. Within its limits, the circle cutter is adjusted quickly to cut different sizes of circular disks or holes in any ordinary material such as wood, fiber, plastic, aluminum, brass or mild steel. Not only that, but by grinding shapes on the cutters you can cut disks with molded edges as in Fig. 2. Or by grinding a shape on the outside edge of the cutter you can cut holes with molded edges. The swinging arm, made from drill rod, carries the cutting bit and must be hardened and drawn on both sizes of the circle cutters detailed. All turning, milling, tapping and broaching must be done first, of course. Broaching required is merely the squaring of the hole taking the larger cutter bit and this can be done with a small file if necessary. The flat on one side of the arm can be milled or ground to size according to the facilities available. Hardening procedure is quite simple. First you heat the part to a cherry red and quench in No. 20 lubricating oil. Clean with fine emery cloth to remove the scale completely. Again heat slowly and uniformly until the metal comes to a light straw color. This temperature is quite critical and the process must be closely watched. At the instant the metal turns uniformly straw color, and before it turns blue, quench in cold water. This process hardens the part sufficiently to prevent the locking setscrew from cutting into the milled surface.

The holder, Fig. 1, is a simple machining job in mild steel. If so desired, the guide pin can

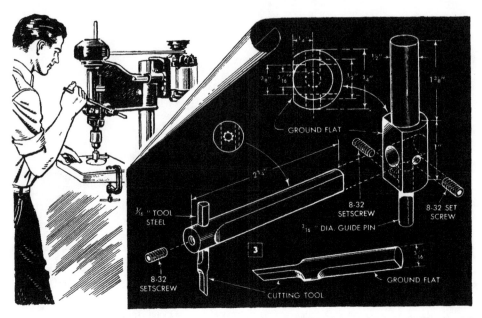

be hardened by the process already described. It will last much longer if hardened. Holes drilled in the holder for the guide pin and the arm carrying the cutting bit are reamed to final size. The groove milled in the body of the holder allows the cutting arm and the bit to slide to within $\frac{5}{16}$ in. of the center of the pilot hole. This brings the minimum hole size that the tool will cut down to $\frac{5}{8}$ in.

The small cutter detailed in Fig. 3 is made up in essentially the same way as the larger size already described. The cutting tool is made from $\frac{3}{16}$-in. drill rod, hardened by heating and quenching. The cutter is not drawn, however. The body of the tool is turned from $\frac{3}{4}$-in. drill rod. A flat is milled or ground on one side of the full-diameter section as shown.

When using circle cutters in the drill press, drive with slowest spindle speed and clamp work securely to the table. Use a cutting oil on steel. Be sure that the pilot hole is the proper diameter and that the cutting tool is adjusted to the proper depth with respect to the guide pin.

Tin Can Serves as Soap Dish In Workshop

For use in the shop or basement where appearance is not too important, a handy soap dish is made from an ordinary tin can. Obtain a fruit-juice can from which the top has not been

removed, and cut it in half lengthwise, leaving a tab on one side as shown. Dull the sharp edges of the metal with a file, and then drill or punch several drain holes in the can and holes in the tab to fasten it to the wall. If you prefer, leave off the tab and punch holes through the ends of the can to suspend it with wire between two faucets on the sink.

Hole in Hammer to Start Nails

When it is necessary to hold both the stock and a nail in position somewhere overhead, or when starting a finishing nail in a spot that is hard to reach, the problem can be solved by using an old hammer that has a hole drilled in

the head to hold the nail. Drill the hole near the edge of the face so it will not interfere with hammering, and make it large enough to accommodate a nail of the largest diameter commonly used. To use, merely insert the nail in the hole, tap it lightly until it grips the wood, and then finish hammering in the normal manner.

BELT SANDER
fits your lathe

DESIGNED to take a standard 6-in. abrasive belt, this lathe sander is an inexpensive unit capable of handling any type of work ordinarily run on a small belt sander. Accurate adjustment for tensioning and tracking is furnished by means of an alignment bar fastened to the underside of the base, which tilts the sander laterally to align the idler with the driving drum, and, at the same time tightens the belt.

Construction should be started by making the two drums. The larger of these— the driving drum — is made from three pieces of 1¾-in. stock, glued and screwfastened together to permit turning as can be seen in Figs. 2 and 4. The drum is fitted on a standard 3-in. faceplate. The idler can be built up similarly or can be turned from a single solid block. Both

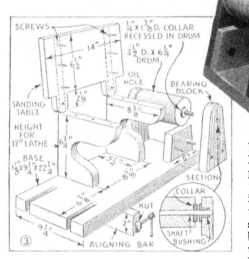

block at one end of the idler is taken off by loosening the wing nuts which hold it in place, Fig. 1. The belt is then slipped over the drums, after which the bearing block is replaced and the nuts tightened. The unit is fitted to the lathe by means of two studs which engage in the slot in the lathe bed. Tension is provided by means of the two screws fitting through the aligning bar. By turning one screw more than the other, proper alignment of the belt for straight tracking is assured. The adjusting screws can be obtained from small C-clamps. The screws are pointed at the free end with a file and engage in shallow holes drilled in the side of the lathe bed. Adjustments are made with the base loosely clamped to the bed, the base bolts being tightened after

drums are 6¼ in. long. Wood stock for the other parts is 1⅛ in. thick with exception of the sander table which is of ¾-in. stock. Because of the short cross grain on the sanding-table supports, Fig. 3, it is advisable to make these of plywood.

To fit the sanding belt in place on the completed unit, the removable bearing

THE 5¼" DRIVING DRUM IS TURNED FROM THREE PIECES OF 1¾" STOCK SCREW-FASTENED TOGETHER

with a hand scrollsaw or coping saw. It consists of a base, a sliding arm and a cam, all made from scrap hardwood stock. Exact sizes are of no importance. You can make it up to suit your work. The arm is faced with a square piece of rubber cut from a stair tread to prevent marring the stock, and the small end slides between a couple of angle-iron brackets to permit adjustment. Also, the cam is pivoted between the brackets. A coil spring fitting tightly in a hole drilled partly through the arm from the underside raises the arm when the cam is released.

tensioning and tracking have been done.

For certain types of work a fence is handy. This is easily cut from scrap stock and attached to the solid bearing support of the idler with screws. It is not shown in the details as most users will want to adapt it to their own special needs. Use a stick belt dressing on the driving drum to prevent slipping of the belt on heavy work. An occasional application will be ample.

This Quick-Acting Clamp Holds Work While Scrollsawing

Here's a clamp that disposes of the problem of holding work for intricate cutting

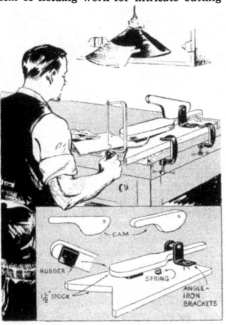

Ball Keeps Stud From Loosening

To keep studs and machine screws from working loose on machinery that is subjected to considerable vibration, recess the bottom end of the stud or screw with a center drill. Then, with a hacksaw, cut two ⅜-in. slots crosswise of the same end. Before driving the stud, drop a steel ball, slightly smaller than the diameter of the stud, into the hole. When the stud is driven in, the ball will expand the recessed end tightly against the sides of the hole, which will hold the stud securely.

Twisted Jigsaw Blades Provide Greater Compass in Sawing

If the saw-blade chucks on your jig-saw are not of the type that can be turned around so that you can feed the work in from one side, you can do this by simply twisting the ends

JIG-SAW BLADE TWISTED

of the blades. Given a half twist at each end the blade will then face sideways when reinserted in the saw chucks. If desired, the blade can be strengthened with a rest of the usual type except that it is notched from the side to support the back of the blade. Be careful to leave enough of the blade straight to allow free movement through the entire length of the stroke.

Homemade BANDSAW for your Workshop

By T. Kasmerchak

THIS bandsaw, made largely of ¼-in. fir plywood, has a 12-in. swing, a tilting table and cuts 2-in. stock with ease and accuracy. If it is carefully constructed, so that both wheels are in perfect alignment, you will have no trouble with the saw blade running off. The cost of building the original saw from which these plans were taken was eight dollars.

For the base and core of the vertical frame piece, Fig. 1, 1⅛-in. yellow pine is used. The pattern for this part is laid out on a piece of heavy wrapping paper, as in Fig. 3. Cut the piece about ⅛ in. oversize, to leave enough stock for finishing. The plywood sides are then cut to size and glued to the core, using casein glue, after which additional strength at the edges is obtained by driving in wood screws. After the glue has dried, the edges of the frame should be sanded on a drum or spindle sander.

The wheels are built up of four 12-in. plywood disks, which are glued together with the grain running crosswise to prevent warping. If desired, the outer, exposed disk may have its center cut out to form a ring. The 6-in. pulley is similarly built up from plywood disks, but the edge,

instead of being flat and covered with a rubber band, should have a V-groove. The hubs for the wheels and pulley are 4-in. ceiling-outlet covers, used in electrical conduit work. Drill a ½-in. hole through the exact center of each, and screw them to the wheels as shown in Figs. 4 and 7, taking care to get them on concentrically. If a ½-in. bolt, with the head

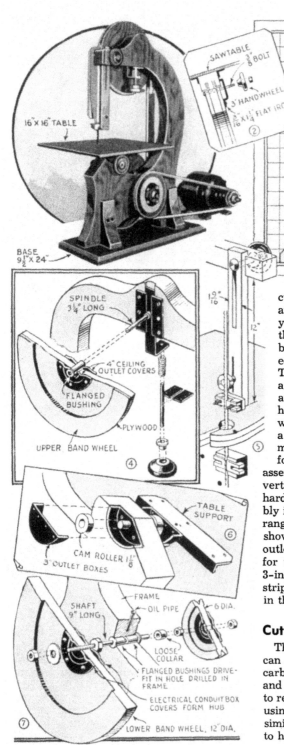

16"×16" TABLE

SAWTABLE
3/8" BOLT

3" HANDWHEEL

3/16" × 1 1/4" FLAT IRON

②

BASE
9 1/2" × 24"

2" SQUARES

③

SPINDLE
3 1/4" LONG

4" CEILING
OUTLET COVERS

FLANGED
BUSHING

PLYWOOD

UPPER BAND WHEEL

④

1 9/16"

12"

⑤

TABLE
SUPPORT

⑥

CAM ROLLER 1 1/8"

3" OUTLET BOXES

FRAME

OIL PIPE

6" DIA.

SHAFT
9" LONG

LOOSE
COLLAR

FLANGED BUSHINGS DRIVE-
FIT IN HOLE DRILLED IN
FRAME

ELECTRICAL CONDUIT BOX
COVERS FORM HUB

⑦

LOWER BAND WHEEL, 12" DIA.

cut off, is slipped through each wheel, and nuts driven tight on each side, you can mount the wheel for turning the diameter true. The wheels should be slightly beveled so that the rear edge is 1/16 in. higher than the front. The saw blade will then tend to run against the thrust wheel of the guide and will not come off. The top wheel has a bearing mounted in the hub, while the lower wheel is fastened to a shaft. Fig. 4 shows the arrangement for adjusting the upper wheel for tension, the bushing and spindle assembly being housed in a slot to allow vertical movement. The adjustable hardwood saw-guide and guard assembly is illustrated in Fig. 5, while the arrangement to make the table tilt is shown in Fig. 6. Three-inch electrical-outlet boxes, cut as indicated, are used for this purpose. Fig. 2 shows how a 3-in. handwheel is turned against a strip of flat iron to hold the saw table in the desired position.

Cutting Edges on Pliers

The cutting edges on a pair of pliers can easily be sharpened with a silicon-carbide stone. First draw the stone back and forth across the edges horizontally to remove nicks. Then sharpen them by using the point of the stone in a manner similar to filing. Care should be taken to hold it at the proper angle.

Flexible-Belt SANDER

Makes Finishing Easy

BUILT of odds and ends easy to get most anywhere, this belt sander will handle practically all sanding operations on flat work of the average size. The design permits a delicate control over the cutting action of the belt and you can see what you're doing, as the work is in full view.

Although you can use any wood or iron pulleys to carry the abrasive belt, Fig. 1 shows how you can make much better pulleys for the purpose right in your own shop. The center section of each pulley is made up of twelve disks of ¼-in. wallboard glued together with casein glue. Then on each side of the center section glue a 1½-in. disk of hardwood, such as birch or maple. After turning, four equally spaced holes are bored through the web of each pulley. These take small stove bolts as in Fig. 1. Now center a hole through the hub of the pulley to take the shaft. The method of keying the pulley to the ¾-in. shaft is also shown. Combining Figs. 1 through 4 you have the story of how the sander is assembled. To carry the pulleys you mount four self-aligning shaft hangers on a hardwood table top, the latter slotted for the V-belt to the motor, and also for the angle-iron stop against which the work is placed. This assembly is mounted on an angle-iron stand made as in Fig. 3, with a hardwood shelf underneath on which the motor is mounted. Fig. 4 gives the details on bolting the iron stand together and also shows how you can

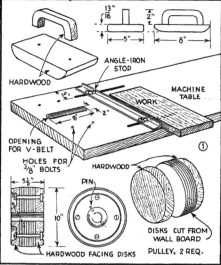

Delicate finish work on small parts, cutting glued-up panels down to uniform thickness, producing a fine finish on veneered panels—all these operations are easy when you have this belt sander. Materials that you do not have at hand to build it are easy to get most anywhere. Lower details show how to make pulleys out of wallboard and hardwood with a friction surface that will prevent slippage of sanding belt

mount the motor on rubber bushings to lessen vibration. Use a rubber V-belt to drive. Speed of the pulleys carrying the sand belt should not exceed 1000 r.p.m. Two small bolts with wing nuts provide the necessary adjustment. The rubbing block is made of hardwood, Fig. 1, with the ends curved upward and the bottom sanded smooth so it does not damage the belt.

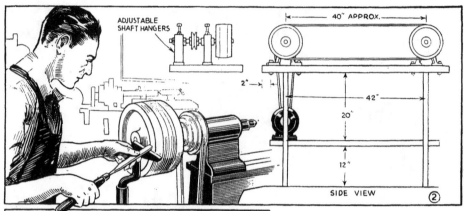

ADJUSTABLE
SHAFT HANGERS

40" APPROX.

2"

42"

20"

12"

SIDE VIEW ②

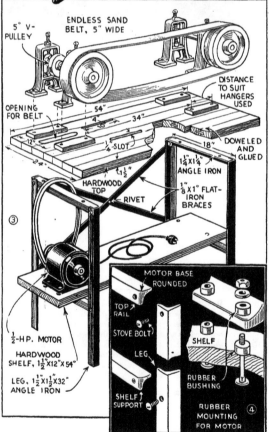

5" V-PULLEY

ENDLESS SAND BELT, 5" WIDE

DISTANCE TO SUIT HANGERS USED

OPENING FOR BELT

54"

4"

34"

12"

¼" SLOT

1¼ X 1¼ ANGLE IRON

18"

DOWELED AND GLUED

2"

1½"

HARDWOOD TOP

RIVET

⅛ X 1" FLAT-IRON BRACES

③

½-HP. MOTOR

HARDWOOD SHELF, 1½" X 12" X 54"

LEG, 1½ X 1½ X 32" ANGLE IRON

MOTOR BASE ROUNDED

TOP RAIL

STOVE BOLT

LEG

SHELF SUPPORT

SHELF

RUBBER BUSHING

RUBBER MOUNTING FOR MOTOR

④

Any sturdy table will do for mounting this sander.
It can be bolted to an open bench, or an angle-iron
stand like that shown above. A ½-hp. motor supplies ample power for any ordinary work. The table
can be made larger than that shown, if you wish to
increase the capacity of the sander

The important thing in using a sander of this type is to keep the work moving in a slow back-and-forth motion across the table while you press the sand belt into contact with the surface. Only a light pressure is needed to insure a fine finish. Suitable endless belts in various grades are available in the length and width required.

Waterproof Glass and Metal Cement

A hard, waterproof adhesive which also will stand fairly high temperatures is made by mixing equal parts of cement and litharge. When these have been mixed, add glycerin in an amount equal to half the volume of powder, and thoroughly mix the paste with a putty knife or spatula. This cement will set under water. and may be used to unite glass or metal parts. To repair leaks in pipes, fill the hole with the cement and bind it in place with cheesecloth. Then daub a quantity of the adhesive on the cloth and wrap the whole thing tightly with even turns of iron wire.

❢A putty that insulates against both heat and electricity can be made by pulverizing sheet asbestos and mixing it to a dough with water glass.

SAW-SANDER UNIT *has tilting tables*

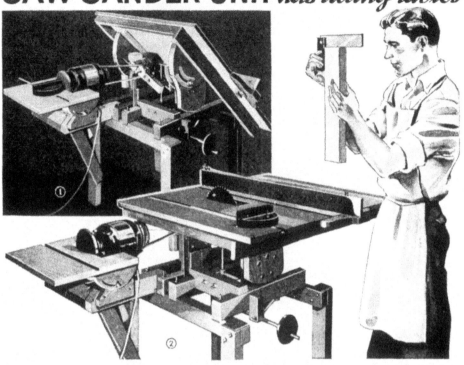

By Carl W. Bertsch

THIS combination workshop unit features an 8-in. saw having a 30 by 36-in. table that will tilt 45 deg., Fig. 1, a swinging saw mandrel, and a direct-drive disk sander. A ⅓-hp. motor operates both machines as shown in Fig. 2.

Construction begins with the stand. From Fig. 7 you can see clearly how it is put together with ¼-in. carriage bolts. All stock measures 2 by 3 in., and note that the upper ends of the legs are notched for rigidity. The position of the two-piece front and rear trunnion supports can be marked at this time, and the holes drilled, but it is best not to bolt them to the stand until after the complete trunnion assembly has been attached. The saw hinge support, detailed in Fig. 5, is set 4⅜ in. in from end of the rails between which it is bolted. Now for the trunnions and their slides. Make these of ¾-in. birch or maple and take pains in laying them out from the pattern given in Fig. 8. The concave edge of the slide must make a perfect rubbing fit with the trunnion, and the curved bolt slot should equal the curve of the trunnion so that the latter will not bind. To the back side of each trunnion and its slide, guides of ⅛-in. hard-pressed board are fitted as shown in Fig. 6. These are cut as indicated to overhang the edge of the trunnions 1 in., forming a lip which overlaps the slide. Use flathead screws for attaching the guides, countersinking the heads flush with the surface. The trunnion-bolt holes through the supports are bored 3⅝₆ in. down from the top. Holes for bolting the slides to the trunnion supports are located by placing the trunnion on its bolt and then with a thin cardboard shim between the slide and the support, center the slide beneath it and clamp the latter temporarily to the support. When you have the slide adjusted so that the trunnion works smoothly, drill four holes through both pieces for ¼-in. bolts. A semi-hard brass strap attached to the edge of each slide to bear against the edge of the trunnion (see side view Fig. 8) takes up the thrust of the table when tilted. In place of the cardboard, thin washers are

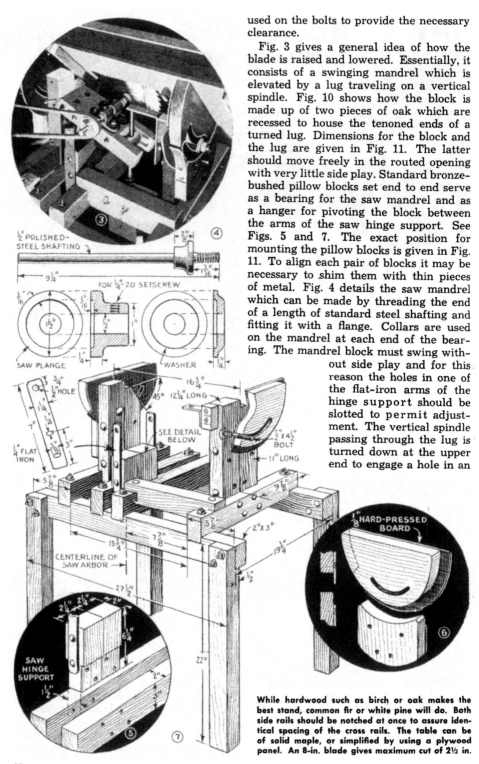

used on the bolts to provide the necessary clearance.

Fig. 3 gives a general idea of how the blade is raised and lowered. Essentially, it consists of a swinging mandrel which is elevated by a lug traveling on a vertical spindle. Fig. 10 shows how the block is made up of two pieces of oak which are recessed to house the tenoned ends of a turned lug. Dimensions for the block and the lug are given in Fig. 11. The latter should move freely in the routed opening with very little side play. Standard bronze-bushed pillow blocks set end to end serve as a bearing for the saw mandrel and as a hanger for pivoting the block between the arms of the saw hinge support. See Figs. 5 and 7. The exact position for mounting the pillow blocks is given in Fig. 11. To align each pair of blocks it may be necessary to shim them with thin pieces of metal. Fig. 4 details the saw mandrel which can be made by threading the end of a length of standard steel shafting and fitting it with a flange. Collars are used on the mandrel at each end of the bearing. The mandrel block must swing without side play and for this reason the holes in one of the flat-iron arms of the hinge support should be slotted to permit adjustment. The vertical spindle passing through the lug is turned down at the upper end to engage a hole in an

While hardwood such as birch or oak makes the best stand, common fir or white pine will do. Both side rails should be notched at once to assure identical spacing of the cross rails. The table can be of solid maple, or simplified by using a plywood panel. An 8-in. blade gives maximum cut of 2½ in.

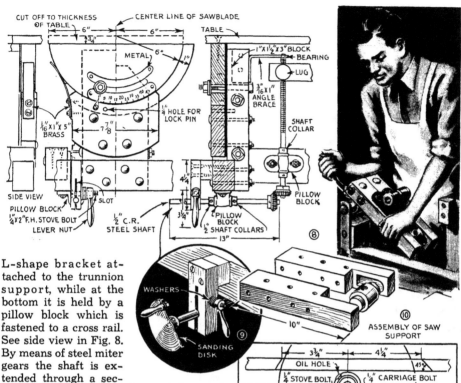

CUT OFF TO THICKNESS OF TABLE — CENTER LINE OF SAWBLADE — TABLE

6" — 6"

3/4"

METAL 6" — 1"

1"X1½"X3" BLOCK — BEARING — LUG

3/16 X 1" ANGLE BRACE

SHAFT COLLAR

¼" HOLE FOR LOCK PIN

1/16"X1"X 5" BRASS — 7⅞"

4¼"

SHAFT COLLAR

PILLOW BLOCK

SIDE VIEW — SLOT

PILLOW BLOCK — ¼X2" F.H. STOVE BOLT LEVER NUT — ½" C.R. STEEL SHAFT — 3¾" — PILLOW BLOCK — ½ SHAFT COLLARS — 13"

⑧

WASHERS

SANDING DISK

⑨

10"

⑩ ASSEMBLY OF SAW SUPPORT

L-shape bracket attached to the trunnion support, while at the bottom it is held by a pillow block which is fastened to a cross rail. See side view in Fig. 8. By means of steel miter gears the shaft is extended through a second pillow block to the front of the stand and fitted with a handwheel which can be made from a small sanding disk. A simple arrangement for locking the shaft is shown in Fig. 9. Now for the table and fence. The former is built up of random widths of maple, using dowels and glue. The blade opening is cut to the size given in Fig. 15 and is fitted with cleats to support a metal insert plate. After this, 3/8 by 3/4-in. grooves are cut in the surface of each side of the blade opening to accommodate a standard miter gauge and then cleats are screwed to the underside as in Fig. 13. The underside of the table above the 2-in. mandrel pulley must be recessed to clear the latter when the blade is raised to its maximum height. The table is attached to each trunnion with three flathead screws, aligning the grooves so that they are parallel with the saw blade. The T-square fence is undercut to ride the table at three points. Figs. 12 and 14 show how bolts and wing nuts are fitted at the front and rear to clamp it in position. With a T-bevel set at known angles, the scale on the front trunnion can be marked for degrees by holding the bevel in contact with the table

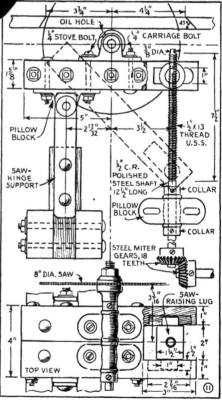

3¾" — 4¼" — 45°

OIL HOLE

¼" STOVE BOLT — ¼" CARRIAGE BOLT

3/8 DIA.

1⅝" — 5" — 1"

7½"

PILLOW BLOCK — 5" — 2 17/32" — 3½"

½" X 13 THREAD U.S.S.

½" C.R. POLISHED STEEL SHAFT 12½" LONG — COLLAR

SAW-HINGE SUPPORT

PILLOW BLOCK — COLLAR

STEEL MITER GEARS, 18 TEETH

8" DIA. SAW — 3 3/16 — SAW-RAISING LUG

4" — 2"

½" — ½"

1"

TOP VIEW — 2 7/8" — 3 3/16"

⑪

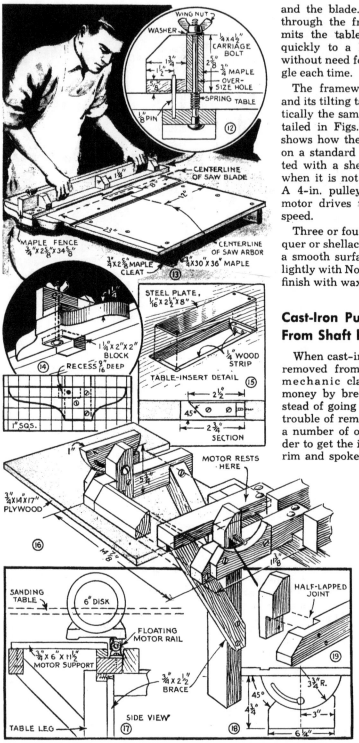

and the blade. A lock pin fitted through the front trunnion permits the table to be returned quickly to a horizontal position without need for checking the angle each time.

The framework of the sander and its tilting table, which is practically the same as the saw, is detailed in Figs. 16 to 19. Fig. 17 shows how the motor is mounted on a standard motor rail and fitted with a shelf on which to set when it is not belted to the saw. A 4-in. pulley on a 1750 r.p.m. motor drives the saw at correct speed.

Three or four coats of clear lacquer or shellac will give the tables a smooth surface. Rub each coat lightly with No. 5-0 sandpaper and finish with wax.

Cast-Iron Pulleys Removed From Shaft by Breaking

When cast-iron pulleys must be removed from a line shaft, one mechanic claims that he saves money by breaking them off instead of going to the expense and trouble of removing the shaft and a number of other pulleys in order to get the iron pulley off. The rim and spokes break easily, and two men can usually break off the hub in a short time. One of them holds an anvil against the top of the hub, while the other uses a sledge hammer on the underside. In this way, there is no danger of springing or otherwise damaging the shaft.

⟨Coils cut from a small coil spring with a cold chisel will serve nicely as lock washers.

Three-wheel BANDSAW has 22-in. throat

4" DIA. HUB

GRAIN OF DISKS AT RIGHT ANGLES

8"

2"

1½"

½"

BICYCLE PEDAL

WOOD SCREW

SETSCREW

1" X 4¾" DRIVE PULLEY

HOLE TO SUIT MOTOR SHAFT

1

WITH its deep throat and sturdy wooden frame, this three-wheel bandsaw handles 4-in. stock with ease and is capable of cutting to the center of a 44-in. disk. Excluding the motor and 80-in. blade, there are no new metal fittings needed, as the blade guide is improvised from a screw-type pulley, and wheel bearings are provided by old bicycle pedals.

After cutting the main frame pieces according to dimensions given in Fig. 2, and assembling them with glue and screws, mark center lines for the two guide wheels. Then, fit drilled-and-tapped plates of steel flush in the upper arm and the center frame member to take bicycle-pedal bearings, which are used for mounting the wheels. As shown in Fig. 1, the guide wheels consist of three ½-in.-wood disks, glued and screwed together with the grain running at right angles to prevent warping. They are trued on a lathe, crowned slightly, and sanded so that vibration is reduced to a minimum, after which 4-in.-dia. hubs are

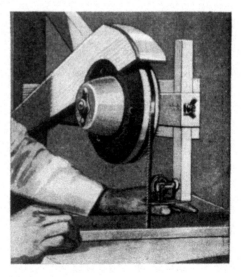

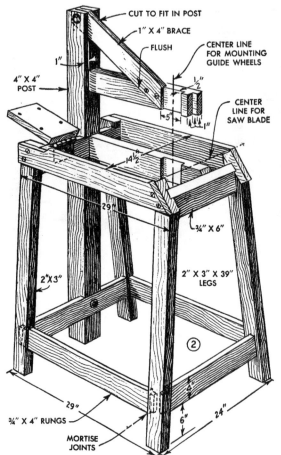

CUT TO FIT IN POST
1" X 4" BRACE
FLUSH
CENTER LINE FOR MOUNTING GUIDE WHEELS
1"
4" X 4" POST
1/2"
CENTER LINE FOR SAW BLADE
5"
1"
4 1/2"
29"
3/4" X 6"
2"X3"
2" X 3" X 39" LEGS
4"
②
29"
3/4" X 4" RUNGS
6"
24"
MORTISE JOINTS

turned, bored and then glued to the outer surfaces of the wheels. These provide spacers to facilitate tightening the bicycle-pedal bearings securely. The drive pulley is turned from a single piece of 1-in. hardwood and fitted with a metal hub, improvised from an old auto-pump pulley or made especially for the purpose. The hub can be attached with either wood screws or small bolts.

Next comes the motor base, which is hinged at the rear of the frame and aligned with the front guide wheels before anchoring the motor securely as shown in Fig. 3. To allow for additional adjustment of the motor, which keeps constant tension on the blade, it's a good idea to cut slots in the base so that the motor can be shifted sideways quickly, if necessary, to get perfect blade trackage.

Fig. 4 shows the table-trunnion assembly, which permits tilting the table to 45 deg. and adjusting it for any angle cuts within this range. Note that the table supports are made by sawing a 5½-in. wooden disk in half and that filler pieces are needed on each side of the frame, the top edges of these being cut to the same contour as the half-round table supports. The important thing here is to position these pieces so that when the table is tilted, the blade will remain in the center of the table opening. By placing a blade on the wheels,

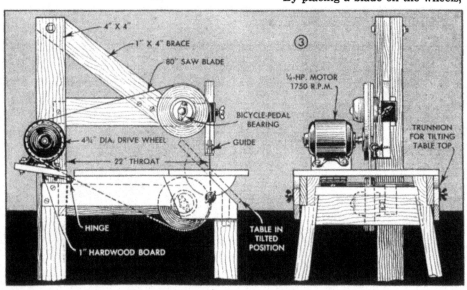

4" X 4"
1" X 4" BRACE
80" SAW BLADE
③
1/4-HP. MOTOR 1750 R.P.M.
BICYCLE-PEDAL BEARING
4¾" DIA. DRIVE WHEEL
GUIDE
TRUNNION FOR TILTING TABLE TOP
22" THROAT
HINGE
1" HARDWOOD BOARD
TABLE IN TILTED POSITION

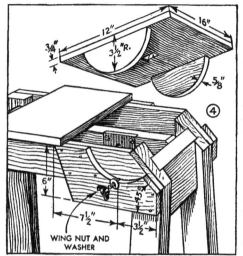

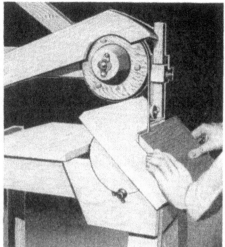

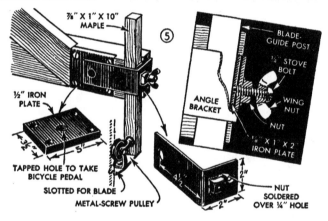

you can determine the correct location easily. Wing nuts and large washers on the trunnion bolts make the table assembly easy to loosen or tighten in any position. If desired, the trunnion also can be indexed for rapid setting.

For the adjustable blade-guide post, Fig. 5, a piece of good maple and a screw-type pulley will be required. After screwing the pulley in place near the lower end of the guide post and fitting the post with a slotted metal plate to take the blade, the vertical adjusting clamp is attached. This consists mainly of an angle bracket made by bending a piece of flat iron and fitting it with a setscrew as indicated. The bracket is drilled to slip over the wheel shaft, and also is anchored at the end of the frame arm with a long, flathead wood screw. Instead of tapping the bracket for an improvised adjusting screw, a nut is soldered over the hole for it as shown.

The lower edge of the upper arm is approximately 15½ in. from the top of the 4 by 4-in. post which is 62 in. in length. The upper detail of Fig. 4 shows the slot through which the blade is inserted or removed. To do this the trunnion must be taken off first and then screwed back on when the blade is in place. The slot should run with the grain of the wood, but although this weakens the piece, the trunnion will reinforce it.

The original model used a motor on which the shaft projected on both sides. On motors having shafts on only one side, the method of mounting the motor as shown may cause the saw blade to run in the wrong direction. In such cases either the motor rotation will have to be reversed by changing the wiring connections inside the motor, which can be done by a competent electrical service man, or the hinged platform on which the motor is held can be attached to the rear of the 4 by 4-in. post, permitting the motor to be turned around end for end. This arrangement requires a longer blade, and it may be helpful to cut slots in the hinged motor support board to permit a greater range of adjustment.

Installation of a suitable wheel-and-blade guard completes the saw, and it's advisable not to start the machine until this guard is in place as it offers protection against accidents in case a blade is broken.

SAFETY REVERSING SWITCH
For Shop Motors

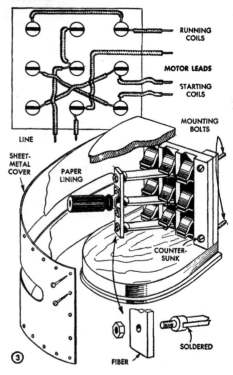

IF YOU use a split-phase or capacitor-type motor in your workshop, you can make a safety reversing switch, Fig. 1, that will enable you to change the rotation of your lathe or drill press without crossing the belt, and in addition you have the protection of an enclosed switch. The unit is made from a t.p.d.t. switch which is cut down to make it more compact. Since the dimensions of switches as manufactured vary, no measurements are given and assembly will have to be by the cut-and-try method. The blades and contacts are removed from the original base and the blades are shortened by cutting them, Fig. 2. To secure the blades to the crossbar, fillister-head screws are slotted and soldered to each blade as shown in the lower detail of Fig. 3. Holes are drilled in the fiber-board crossbar to receive the screws, and the handle is attached by fastening it to a strip of metal which, in turn, is mounted on the crossbar bridging the center blade. The base also is made of fiber board grooved to fit the contacts. These should be spaced as closely as possible, but not so closely that there would be possibility of a short circuit. Also, keep in mind that the location of the contacts must fit the throw of the switch. Top and bottom are of wood curved so the crossbar has clearance to swing within the cover and rabbeted as indicated in the lower detail of Fig. 3. For a cover, sheet metal lined with paper for insulation is used. The slot for the handle is made by drilling a hole at each end and completing the cut with tin shears. When the unit is assembled, label the two closed positions of the switch "Forward" and "Reverse," with the open position marked "Off." Do not change rotation without allowing the motor to stop. The switch can be given the finish as shown so that it is easily seen. A wiring diagram is shown in the upper detail of Fig. 3.

Drive Your HACKSAW
Electrically

ANY ordinary hacksaw frame with the handle removed can be fitted to this simple drive unit, making an efficient power hacksaw that will handle all kinds of light and medium work.

Fig. 1 shows side and end views of the table and gives you a general idea of the assembly. You don't have to be particular about the dimensions of the table. The main thing is rigidity and sufficient weight to absorb vibration of the reciprocating parts. A ¼-hp. motor supplies the power through two sets of reducing pulleys, which bring the speed of the saw down to about 90 strokes per minute. The length of ¾-in. shafting which

Any ordinary hand hacksaw can be used with this simple power drive. The saw frame is clamped to support arm, which is weighted

---

Rubber Heels Cushion Motor

To reduce vibration of electric motors to a minimum, shock-absorbing motor mounts for floating-type rails can be made from a pair of rubber heels. Cut a metal plate to fit the recess in the top of the heel and drill two holes through the heel and plate to line up with rail clips. Countersink the flathead bolts in the plate and bolt the three together. Fasten the heels to the bench with three screws or bolts, using washers under the heads.

supports the intermediate and top pulleys turns in sets of ¾-in. babbitted split bearings. Note that setscrew collars are used on each shaft. One face of the top or driving pulley is fitted with a counterbalancing steel plate as in Figs. 2 and 3. The counterbalance is bolted to the pulley. Construction of the crankpin is shown in Fig. 3, the lower right detail. A section of ½-in. brass rod is threaded on both ends and screwed into a tapped hole in one end of the counterbalance and through the pulley. This crankpin is secured with a nut at the back of the pulley. A ¼-in. pipe tee which has been reamed to fit

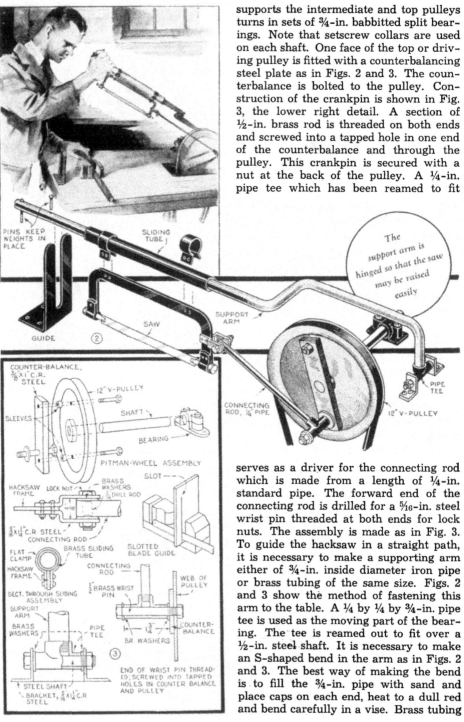

The support arm is hinged so that the saw may be raised easily

serves as a driver for the connecting rod which is made from a length of ¼-in. standard pipe. The forward end of the connecting rod is drilled for a ⁵⁄₁₆-in. steel wrist pin threaded at both ends for lock nuts. The assembly is made as in Fig. 3. To guide the hacksaw in a straight path, it is necessary to make a supporting arm either of ¾-in. inside diameter iron pipe or brass tubing of the same size. Figs. 2 and 3 show the method of fastening this arm to the table. A ¼ by ¼ by ¾-in. pipe tee is used as the moving part of the bearing. The tee is reamed out to fit over a ½-in. steel shaft. It is necessary to make an S-shaped bend in the arm as in Figs. 2 and 3. The best way of making the bend is to fill the ¾-in. pipe with sand and place caps on each end, heat to a dull red and bend carefully in a vise. Brass tubing can be bent cold. The surface of the pipe which supports the hacksaw guide should be polished smooth. The slide is a length of brass tubing which will telescope over the polished section of the supporting arm. The hacksaw frame is fastened to the guide with the aid of clamps as in Fig. 2. These can be riveted to the saw frame or held with small bolts.

The pressure applied to the blade when cutting is regulated by weights on the outer end of the supporting arm as shown in Fig. 1. These weights can be made by drilling a hole in cold-rolled-steel plate of such a size that the piece will slip easily over the pipe. Setscrews or pins can be

By filling the tubing with sand and plugging the ends you can bend it easily

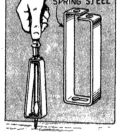

the vise guides the saw blade. The guide plate is fastened to one vise jaw with machine screws. Fig. 4 shows the assembly of the speed-reducing drive. All pulleys are of the V-type for ½-in. belt.

used to hold the weights in place. Different materials require slight variations in blade pressure for the best cutting action. The support-arm guide, Fig. 3, can be made from ¼-in. flat iron, the slot being of the same width as the diameter of the pipe. If necessary, the guide should be blocked up on the bench, so that the arm will reach the bottom of the slot just as the saw breaks through the work.

A standard toolmakers' vise can be used to hold the work. A slotted plate fitted in

Screw Holder For Screwdriver

Shaped from a piece of thin spring steel, this attachment will enable you to start screws in places where it is impossible to reach with the hands. A slot with a hole at one end permits a screw head to be inserted and held true for starting it straight.

Electric VIBRATING "PENCIL"
tools soft metals

By C. A. Crowley

THIS handy engraving "pencil" engraves name plates, initials tools, lays out metal templates, and is useful for tooling craftwork of all kinds. It operates on 110-volt 60-cycle alternating current, and will not work on direct current.

An electromagnet is the heart of the tool. Its core consists of E-stampings from an old audio-frequency radio transformer, dimensions of which are shown in Fig. 3, although these are not extremely critical. The number of turns required for the coil is equal to 493 divided by the cross-sectional area of the core. The cross-sectional area of the core is the width of the center

leg on which the coil is to be wound, multiplied by the thickness. In the case of the core shown, the center leg is .25 sq. in. The number of turns required is therefore 493 divided by .25, or 1972.

The wire size is calculated from the length of the magnetic path, as shown in the upper detail of Fig. 7. The wire size in circular mils is found by multiplying the

length by 50,000, and then dividing by the number of turns. For a magnetic path of 3¼ in., the wire size required is 3.25 times 50,000, divided by 1972, or 82.5 circular mils. The required gauge number is then found from any magnet wire table, which will show that No. 31 has an area of 80 circular mils, and No. 30 has an area of 101 circular mils. In such a case, the larger

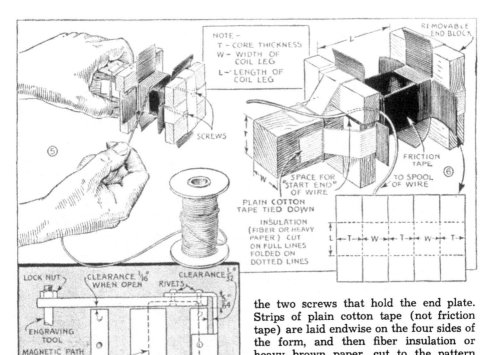

NOTE –
T – CORE THICKNESS
W – WIDTH OF COIL LEG
L – LENGTH OF COIL LEG

SCREWS

⑤

REMOVABLE END BLOCK

FRICTION TAPE
⑥

SPACE FOR "START END" OF WIRE

TO SPOOL OF WIRE

PLAIN COTTON TAPE TIED DOWN

INSULATION (FIBER OR HEAVY PAPER) CUT ON FULL LINES FOLDED ON DOTTED LINES

LOCK NUT
CLEARANCE 1/16" WHEN OPEN
CLEARANCE 1/32"
RIVETS

ENGRAVING TOOL
MAGNETIC PATH THROUGH CORE AND ARMATURE

DRILLED AND TAPPED FOR ENGRAVING TOOL
FLAT-HEAD RIVETS COUNTERSUNK

A.C. ONLY ELECTRIC RAZOR
SHAFT THREADED
3/4" LONGER THAN CORE
LOCK NUTS
1/2 x 7/8 COLD-ROLLED STEEL ARMATURE
CUTTING HEAD REMOVED
#16 C.R. STEEL
SHANK FLATTENED AND TAPPED
⑦
CORE THICKNESS
DRILLED FOR RIVETS

size (lower gauge number) should be chosen. The coil will, therefore, be wound with 1972 turns of No. 30 enameled wire. As most audio-frequency transformers are close to the dimensions given, No. 30 wire is satisfactory, but where a heavy-duty outfit is to be built from larger E-stampings, larger wire will be necessary.

The coil is wound on a wooden form as shown in Figs. 5 and 6. The form should be slightly larger than the leg on which the coil fits, and should also have a slight taper toward the end, so that the finished coil can be slipped off readily after removing

the two screws that hold the end plate. Strips of plain cotton tape (not friction tape) are laid endwise on the four sides of the form, and then fiber insulation or heavy brown paper, cut to the pattern shown in Fig. 6, is laid over the form and held in place with a single band of friction tape. Wind the coil tightly and evenly, avoiding all kinks. When the coil is finished, tie the cotton tapes tightly over the coil and remove the coil from the form. Wrap a single band of friction tape around each side of the coil. The leads from the coil should be soldered to a suitable length of lampcord, and the soldered joints taped. Then the coil can be slipped on the core and held in place with a small wood wedge.

The armature assembly shown in Figs. 4 and 7 is constructed of cold-rolled steel. The armature is fastened to its bracket with two flathead rivets, countersunk in the armature. Clearances and dimensions specified should be followed carefully.

Engraving tools can be made of 1/8-in. or larger drill rod. The tips can be ground to various shapes, as shown in Fig. 2. After rough-grinding to shape, the ends should be hardened by heating to a straw-yellow color and plunging the cutting end only into cold water. After hardening they are finish ground. The shank of the tool can be threaded and screwed into the end of the armature; a lock nut and lock washer are used to hold them firmly. If a single engraving bit is to be used, it can be held permanently in place by peening.

The completed tool can be mounted on a semicircular wooden block, and placed inside a fiber tube. See Figs. 1 and 4.

Another way to make a simple engraving tool is to take an inexpensive vibrator-type (labeled a.c. only) electric razor, of the kind which contains an electromagnet instead of a motor. See the left detail of Fig. 7. Remove the cutter head from the shaver and, if necessary, saw off the end of the Bakelite case. An engraving tool can be attached to the vibrating shaft of the shaver.

One way to do this is to swage the shank of the tool flat, and drill it to fit the shaft. It can be held in place by peening, or the shaft can be threaded and the tool tapped and held with a lock nut.

Jackshaft on Motor Makes Variable-Speed Unit

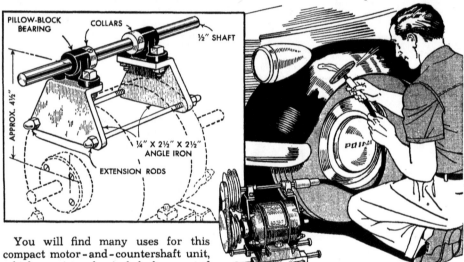

You will find many uses for this compact motor-and-countershaft unit, which consists of a jackshaft mounted on an electric motor. The unit can be fastened in a fixed position for driving power tools, such as metal-turning lathes, drill presses, etc., where various speeds are required, or it can be carried about for operating a flexible shaft as shown. By using two 5-in. cone pulleys and a motor of 1750 r.p.m. on the original unit a speed range of 700 to 4375 r.p.m. was obtained.

Pillow blocks serve as bearings for the shaft, and they are bolted to angle-iron supports, which are attached to the motor by placing them under the nuts of the tie rods that hold the motor housing together. In some cases, it may be necessary to substitute longer tie rods for the original ones.

Kent H. Alverson, Niagara Falls, N. Y.

Small Paper Cups Have Many Uses in the Home Workshop

An inexpensive convenience in your home workshop is a supply of small paper cups. They are particularly handy when doing small jobs of finishing, or in mixing paints and stains. When tin cans are used for this purpose they always must be cleaned for the next job, and frequently bits of skins or traces of the old color remain. But paper cups are merely thrown away when a job is finished. Labels and measures can be marked on them easily with a pencil, and liquid levels show clearly through the translucent sides.

❡To remove rust from the flutes of an auger bit use a small rope which is coated with glue or shellac and sprinkled with fine emery.

Metal-Turning TOOL SLIDE fits Your Wood Lathe

by W. R. Bell.....

A NY good wood-turning lathe may be used for metal turning, boring, milling and facing with the addition of this compound tool slide. It is easily made from cold-rolled steel with a few common tools.

Make two each of the upper and lower cross slides shown in Figs. 1 and 2, the parts being clamped together while drilling the holes for screws, which hold the assembly together. Means of attaching the lower cross slide to the lathe bed must be worked out to suit the individual lathe. Fig. 4 gives suggested mountings for the more common types of lathe beds, the parts being screwed together. In each case, the mounting consists of a hold-down screw or stud, a key for alignment and a spacer block. The block should be ½ in. thick for lathes having an 8-in. swing, 1 in. for a 9-in. swing, and proportionately thicker for larger

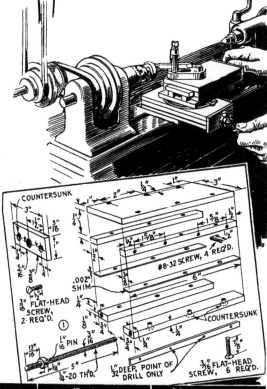

Turning

Boring

Facing

Milling

sizes. For a 7-in. swing, omit the block and attach the key and stud directly to the bottom surface of the lower slide.

Fig. 5 shows the swivel arrangement for making angular cuts, using two metal disks. The handles shown for the lead screws may be replaced by turned handles and dial indicators, which can be marked in thousandths of an inch, as the 20 threads per inch on the lead screws permit .050-in. movement of the slide for each complete turn of the screw. Thus, fifty equal spaces on the longitudinal dial and one hundred equal spaces on the cross-slide dial will give .001-in. cut at the tool. The reason for twice as many marks on the cross slide is

79

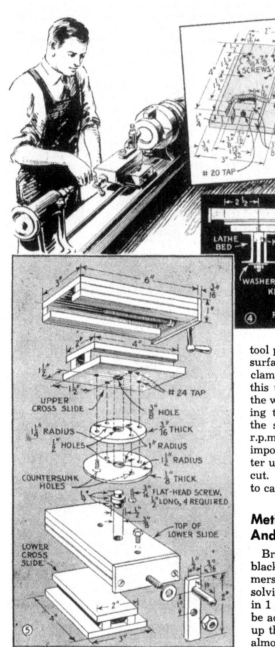

tool post and holder, Fig. 3, permit the top surface of the slide to be cleared for clamping down work to be milled. For this use, the spindle rotation is reversed, the work is fed with the cutter teeth pushing toward the travel and pressure, and the speed is reduced greatly. About 60 r.p.m. works well with small cutters. It is important that the work be fed to the cutter uniformly throughout the length of the cut. Any irregularity in the feed is likely to cause breakage.

Method for Bluing And Blackening Brass Ware

Brass articles may be given a blue or black color by first cleaning and then immersing them in a solution made by dissolving hypo, ½ lb., and lead acetate, 2 oz., in 1 gal. of water. More lead acetate may be added to deepen the color and to speed up the action. To use the solution, heat it almost to the boiling point and immerse the work, watching carefully to remove it when the color is of a suitable shade. Brass wire should be used to suspend the work in the solution, and the finished work should be protected with clear lacquer to preserve the finish.

due to the fact that a half-thousandth cut on the radius reduces the diameter of the work twice that amount. The swivel turret may also be marked or scribed in degrees for accurate work. The removable

Bench Stop With Clamping-Bar Members Has "Gripping" Action When Holding Work

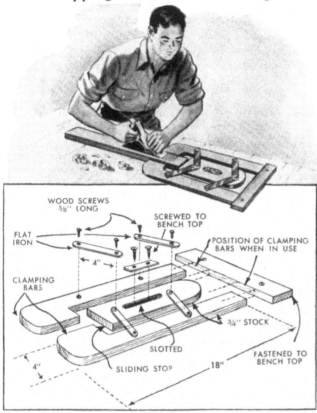

WOOD SCREWS ⅝" LONG

SCREWED TO BENCH TOP

FLAT IRON

POSITION OF CLAMPING BARS WHEN IN USE

CLAMPING BARS

← 4" →

¾" STOCK

SLOTTED

SLIDING STOP

FASTENED TO BENCH TOP

4"

18"

Made from two clamping bars, a sliding member or stop and a fixed piece, this bench stop adjusts itself automatically to various widths, and holds the work in a vise-like grip. Only a few general dimensions are given; the others can be determined by the size of the work to be handled. Remember that the length of the flat-iron pieces to which the clamping bars pivot, will determine the width of boards that the stop will take. After the bars and sliding member have been cut out of ¾-in. hardwood stock, assemble them as shown in the detail, fastening the pivots to the bars and the stop with wood screws ⅝ in. long. Then fasten the fixed piece in place and determine the position of the sliding stop. When this is located, screw it in place using flatheaded wood screws and a length of flat iron drilled for the screws. As the unit is fastened to the bench by only four screws, it is easy to remove.

Jig Aids in Boring Small Bushings

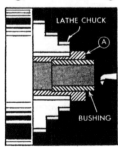

LATHE CHUCK

A

BUSHING

When it is necessary to enlarge the hole in a small bushing exactly concentric with the outside diameter, this boring jig will save time and afford greater accuracy than mounting the bushing directly in the lathe chuck. Bore a hole in a short length of brass or soft-steel rod to a push fit over the bushing, detail A. If you wish, leave a small internal shoulder to back up the bushing, but be sure it will not interfere with pushing out the work. Then, insert the bushing in the sleeve, allowing it to project a short distance, and chuck the assembly. Light cuts with the boring bar at a fairly high speed will do an accurate job.

Drill and Tap for Cast Iron Combined in One Tool

Made from a 4-fluted high-speed tap, this combination tool permits drilling and tapping through cast iron in one operation. Grind off the threads about halfway up from the bottom of the

END VIEW

THREADS GROUND OFF

TWO FLUTES GROUND DOWN

tap and grind off two opposite flutes, forming cutting edges so this portion of the tap will serve as a drill. To use, chuck the tool in a drill press and bore through the work until the threads are reached. Then tap the hole by turning in the remaining half of the tool by hand. This tool has been used successfully on cast iron up to ⁹⁄₁₆ in. thick.

Charles N. Dyer, Kansas City, Mo.

Fence and Table Extension Improve Bandsaw

By Edward R. Lucas

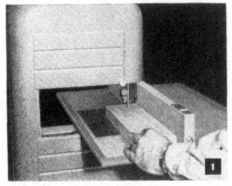

The photos above and below show the bandsaw-table extension being used for straight and bevel cuts

An enlarged working area and provision for a long rip fence are advantages of this bandsaw-table extension. The fence is shown in use in Fig. 1, and Fig. 2 shows the table tilted for a bevel cut. Because sizes of bandsaw tables and throats vary, no overall dimensions are given; the extension must be made to suit the saw being used. Fig. 3 shows how the parts are cut and assembled. The table extension consists of a piece of plywood having edges faced with solid stock. These are tongue-and-groove joints glued flush with the surface of the plywood. The opening for the bandsaw table is jigsawed for a snug fit. Four cleats are screwed around the opening on the underside and holes are drilled in them for 1/4-in. bolts. Matching holes are drilled and tapped in the sides of the bandsaw table, and the extension is attached to the table with bolts through these holes. Next, add the beveled guide rails for the rip fence and cut the slot for the saw blade, being sure that it is aligned with the slot in the metal table. The rip fence is detailed in Fig. 3. Note that the guide blocks are grooved to fit the guide rails and attached to the end pieces by half-lapped joints. Then one end piece is screwed to the fence and the other is hinged and drilled for a hanger bolt and wing nut for clamping the fence in place. The lower right-hand detail shows how the fence is assembled.

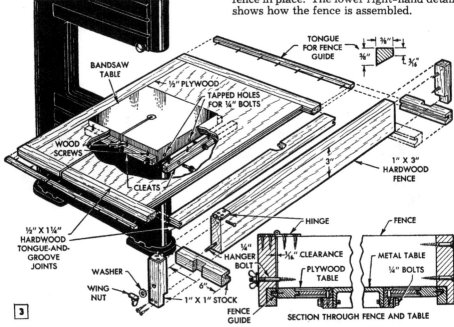

Homemade WOOD LATHE
mounted on floor stand

Self-contained unit has four-speed V-belt drive, rigid iron bed, and a quick-acting tailstock

WITH this lathe you can swing a disk 12 in. in diameter on the headstock or turn down a full-length table leg between centers. The headstock spindle, Fig. 1, is supported on auto connecting rods bolted to a short length of channel which forms the base and is bolted to the bed. A hardwood spacer between the rods holds the whole thing rigid. The ½-in. spindle runs in brass spindle-bolt bushings which are pressed into the upper ends of the connecting rods and then reamed to give the spindle a free-running fit. The spindle also carries two ball thrust bearings, one on each side of a four-step V-pulley. Polished flat washers are used to take out the end play, if any. The inner end of the spindle should project about ¾ in. to take a hollow-sleeve spur center of the type which locks in place with a headless setscrew. This and the drive pulley, also the thrust bearings, can be purchased at little cost. Faceplates are also available.

The bed is simply two channels of the size given in Fig. 3. They are bolted together with spacers cut from pipe, the latter of such length as to leave the top flanges of the channels exactly 1 in. apart when the bolts are drawn tight. Now, the stand consists of two end members joined directly to the bed as in Fig. 3, and to a lower shelf as in Fig. 4. The motor shelf is assembled from three pieces of 1½-in. angle as in Fig. 3. It's a good idea to make up the stand first, then

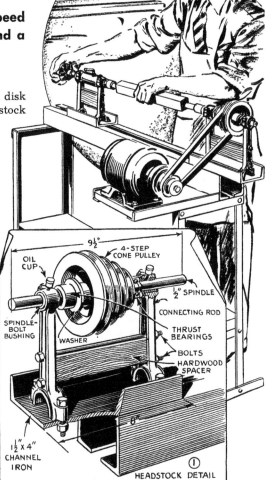

HEADSTOCK DETAIL ①

cut these pieces to suit the motor and V-belt you are to use. Fig. 2 shows a trick in fitting angle iron that should be used in building this stand, as it results in a rigid joint. After the pieces are cut to required length, file one end of the angle which meets the corner of the second angle, in this case the leg, to a contour which allows it to fit snugly, clamp the pieces together,

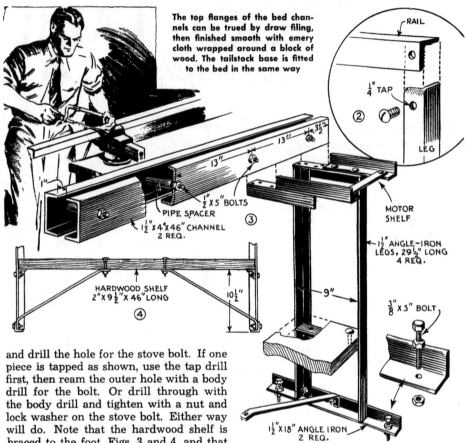

The top flanges of the bed channels can be trued by draw filing, then finished smooth with emery cloth wrapped around a block of wood. The tailstock base is fitted to the bed in the same way

RAIL

¼" TAP

②

LEG

13"

3¼"

13"

½" X 5" BOLTS

PIPE SPACER

③

1½" X 4" X 46" CHANNEL
2 REQ.

MOTOR
SHELF

1½" ANGLE-IRON
LEGS, 29½" LONG
4 REQ.

HARDWOOD SHELF
2" X 9½" X 46" LONG

10½"

9"

④

⅜" X 3" BOLT

1½" X 18" ANGLE IRON
2 REQ.

and drill the hole for the stove bolt. If one piece is tapped as shown, use the tap drill first, then ream the outer hole with a body drill for the bolt. Or drill through with the body drill and tighten with a nut and lock washer on the stove bolt. Either way will do. Note that the hardwood shelf is braced to the foot, Figs. 3 and 4, and that the shelf rests on an angle-iron rail to which it is bolted. Foot pieces of 1½-in. angle are bolted to the ends of the legs. A machine bolt or cap screw is put through near the ends of each foot piece and held in any position with two nuts, one on each side of one leg of the angle as shown. This gives adjustment for leveling the lathe on an uneven floor.

Finally, the tailstock and tool rest. Fig. 6 suggests a method of making the latter. You can purchase this item ready-made also. Figs. 5 and 7 show clearly how the tailstock is made. As you will see, it is very similar to the headstock. The quill is turned out of 1-in. cold-rolled-steel shafting, the ends being shouldered back the length and diameter of the upper connecting-rod bearings, leaving a center section 4½ in. long. The quill is counterbored as shown and a portion tapped to take the

threaded section of the spindle. The locking device consists of a cam rolling in slots cut in the channel-iron base as in Fig. 7 and actuated by a ball handle. The cam is made by filing slots in a piece of ¾-in. shafting. These slots cause the shaft to move eccentrically, lifting the U-bolt and the plate which bind against the flanges of the bed and tighten the tailstock at any position.

A ¼-hp. motor of 1750 r.p.m. will furnish sufficient power for ordinary work. By using matched 4-step cone pulleys on motor and headstock you will not have to shift the motor to change the spindle speed. By making up hinged motor rails from strips of hardwood or ¼-in. flat iron it will be much easier to shift the belt when changing speeds. Hinged motor rails can also be purchased ready-made.

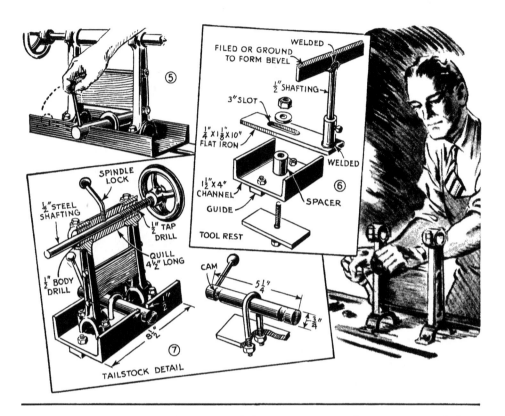

⑤

WELDED
FILED OR GROUND
TO FORM BEVEL

$\frac{1}{2}$" SHAFTING

3" SLOT

$\frac{1}{4}$" X 1$\frac{1}{8}$" X 10"
FLAT IRON

1$\frac{1}{2}$" X 4"
CHANNEL

GUIDE

TOOL REST

WELDED

⑥

SPACER

SPINDLE
LOCK

$\frac{1}{2}$" STEEL
SHAFTING

$\frac{1}{2}$" TAP
DRILL

QUILL
4$\frac{1}{2}$" LONG

$\frac{1}{2}$" BODY
DRILL

CAM

5$\frac{1}{4}$"

$\frac{3}{4}$"

8$\frac{1}{2}$"

⑦

TAILSTOCK DETAIL

This Lathe Sanding Table Fits Tool-Post Holder

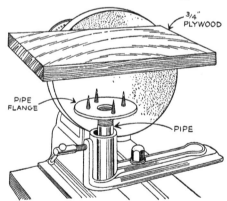

$\frac{3}{4}$"
PLYWOOD

PIPE
FLANGE

PIPE

When squaring up small pieces of stock on a lathe sanding disk it is very often an advantage to have a table that can be adjusted easily and quickly to the best working height in relation to the disk. Made from a piece of plywood of a convenient size, a short length of pipe and a flange, you have a table that is adjustable both vertically and horizontally. The tool-rest base forms the holder, and the sanding table is held in the desired position by simply running up the clamp screw.

GRINDING JIG for TOOL BITS

1

By Walter T. Warde

EVERY experienced machinist knows just how near to the impossible it is to grind the three angles on a lathe or shaper tool bit correctly by hand. Perhaps one, or maybe two, can be done freehand with fair accuracy, but three angles—that's too big an order in most good shops. A better and surer way is to make a grinding jig such as that detailed in Fig. 2. This jig gives the necessary movement in three planes, one each for the cutting angle, the side clearance angle and the front clearance angle successively. Calibrations indicate the various angle settings accurately. Although it's not to be classed as a precision tool this jig will be found practical for grinding lathe and shaper bits for ordinary work. To make the three principal parts of the jig use a material that mills well. The base, Fig. 2, slides in a guide as in Fig. 1. The swiveling member, which supports the toolholder, is calibrated through a 50-deg. included angle for grinding side clearance. The base calibration of 80 deg. provides for grinding the cutting angle, while the 35-deg. calibration of the toolholder takes care of the front clearance angle. However, calibration for the latter is correct only when grinding on the side of the wheel. When grinding on the face of the wheel the jig must be lowered so that the tool bit contacts the wheel at a point exactly in line laterally with its axis. Otherwise the correct grinding angle must be calculated. This can be done by sketching an enlarged section of the wheel and toolholder and then plotting the required angle setting.

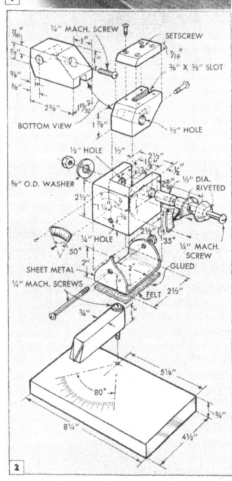

2

High-Speed HAND GRINDER
carves, drills and polishes

By A. L. Mills

BUILT around a small motor of the type used in high-speed electrical appliances, the sturdy hand grinder shown in Fig. 1, when fitted with a collet chuck to take small carving bits and accessories, makes a versatile workshop tool. Essentially, the job consists of adding an extension shaft and·housing to the motor and providing a handle.

The steel shaft is machined to the size detailed in Fig. 2. One end is turned to accommodate a standard collet chuck, while the other end is fitted with a short tight-fitting pin to engage a slotted spring coupling. Standard magneto-type ball bearings are used to support the shaft inside the 1⅜-in. steel tube. The rear bearing is mounted 1¼ in. from the end and is bushed with shim brass to a press fit inside the tubing, after which the bearing is soldered permanently in place. The front bearing is likewise shimmed, but is held in place with liquid solder to make the shaft removable for future bearing re-

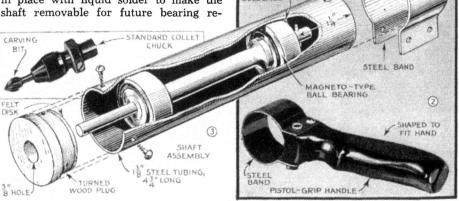

placement and inspection. When this is necessary the solder is loosened with a knife to free the bearing. A rabbeted hardwood plug, backed with a felt disk, is turned to fit snugly in the end of the tubing flush with the outside and is fastened in place with three short wood screws as shown in Fig. 3.

Fig. 4 shows a simple universal shaft

coupling which consists of a short length of brass tubing soldered to each end of a heavy coil spring. This is pinned permanently to the motor shaft after a small fan, formed from a sheet-brass disk as in Fig. 6, is fastened to the shaft close to the motor. The opposite end of the coupling is slotted to engage the cross pin in the extension shaft.

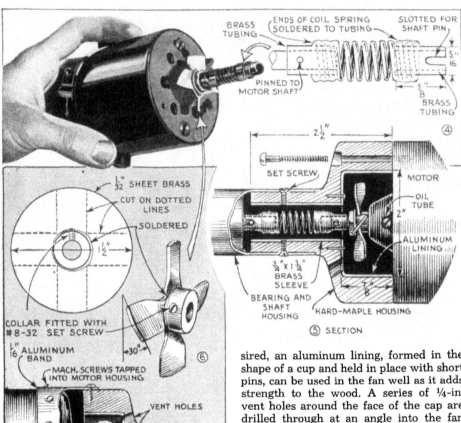

ENDS OF COIL SPRING (SOLDERED TO TUBING)

BRASS TUBING

SLOTTED FOR SHAFT PIN

$\frac{5}{16}$"

PINNED TO MOTOR SHAFT

$\frac{5}{8}$"

BRASS TUBING

④

$2\frac{1}{2}$"

SET SCREW

MOTOR

OIL TUBE

2"

ALUMINUM LINING

$\frac{3}{4}$" X $1\frac{3}{4}$" BRASS SLEEVE

BEARING AND SHAFT HOUSING

HARD-MAPLE HOUSING

⑤ SECTION

$\frac{1}{32}$" SHEET BRASS

CUT ON DOTTED LINES

SOLDERED

$1\frac{1}{2}$"

COLLAR FITTED WITH #8-32 SET SCREW

$\frac{1}{16}$" ALUMINUM BAND

30°

MACH. SCREWS TAPPED INTO MOTOR HOUSING

⑥

VENT HOLES

$1\frac{1}{4}$"

METHOD OF ATTACHING HOUSING TO ROUND-NOSE MOTOR

$1\frac{1}{2}$"

⑦

A counterbored hardwood cap, to which the bearing-and-shaft assembly is fastened, must be made to fit the motor. Figs. 5 and 7 show two methods of attaching the cap to a motor. In the method shown in Fig. 7, it is important not to drill and tap setscrew holes into the field coils of the motor. Regardless of the method used, the counterboring of the cap in either case is identical. Fig. 5 details how the extension is fastened solidly to the cap by means of oval-headed setscrews drawn up tightly in holes tapped through the side of a brass sleeve inserted in one end. If de-

sired, an aluminum lining, formed in the shape of a cup and held in place with short pins, can be used in the fan well as it adds strength to the wood. A series of $\frac{1}{4}$-in. vent holes around the face of the cap are drilled through at an angle into the fan well to admit air to the motor.

The pistol-grip handle shown in Fig. 2, is shaped to fit the hand and is attached to the shaft extension at about the center of balance. It is important that the shaft turns clockwise, especially when the unit is to be used for drilling and carving.

Here Is an Easy Method Of Bending Plywood

If you have had difficulty in bending plywood, try the following method: First wet both sides of the wood and then go over it with a hot smoothing iron, preferably an electric one, which is hot enough to convert the moisture to steam. Go over each side of the board twice in this manner. Then, as the wood is being bent, apply the hot iron to the wet surface as the arc is formed. Quarter-inch fir plywood may be bent around a 4-in. radius without cracking.

⟪A countersink is a good emergency tool for splitting and clinching tubular rivets.

Homemade SHAPER
has ball-bearing spindle

By Albert C. Larson

WITH this shaper set up ready for work you are independent of the limitations of stock moldings, for, with an assortment of cutters you can make practically any molded shape you may require in a few minutes.

The greater part of the story on construction of the spindle is told in Figs. 2, 3 and 4. The spindle assembly is housed in a 5-in. length of brass or steel tubing. This length is only an approximation for you may have to file the ends back slightly to get proper fit of the retaining washers. Note especially from Fig. 2 that there is an inner tube which acts as a bearing spacer and that between this and the housing proper is a light sheet-metal shim. The shim extends beyond the ends of the housing and the whole thing is held in

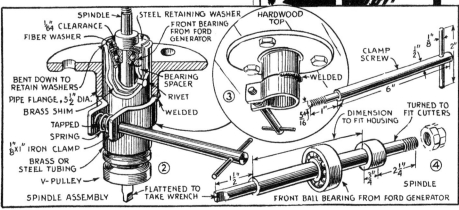

place with a rivet. The housing is also drilled and tapped for a pressure grease fitting.

Right at this stage the spindle, Fig. 4, should be made. Check the dimension through each of the inner ball races before you turn down the spindle between the cutter flange and the shouldered lower end, for this section must fit the inner ball races in a snug, press fit. Thread the upper end of the spindle while in the lathe as the thread must be true. When you assemble as in Fig. 2 make sure, before seating the retainer, that the spindle turns freely, without perceptible binding at any point, through a complete revolution.

Next, you bore out the threaded sleeve of a pipe floor flange so that the spindle

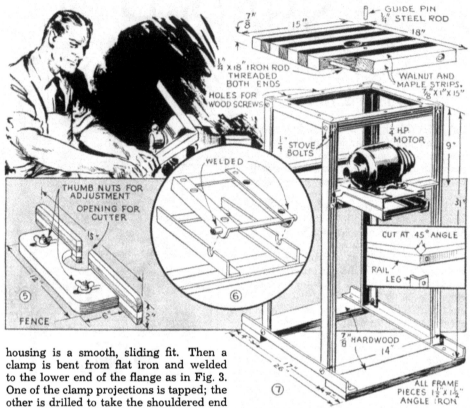

GUIDE PIN ¼" STEEL ROD

¼ X 18" IRON ROD THREADED BOTH ENDS

HOLES FOR WOOD SCREWS

WALNUT AND MAPLE STRIPS ⅞" X 1" X 15"

¼ H.P. MOTOR

¼" STOVE BOLTS

WELDED

THUMB NUTS FOR ADJUSTMENT

OPENING FOR CUTTER

CUT AT 45° ANGLE

RAIL

LEG

FENCE

⑤

⑥

⑦

⅞" HARDWOOD 14"

ALL FRAME PIECES 1½" X 1½" ANGLE IRON

housing is a smooth, sliding fit. Then a clamp is bent from flat iron and welded to the lower end of the flange as in Fig. 3. One of the clamp projections is tapped; the other is drilled to take the shouldered end of the clamp screw, Fig. 4. A coil spring is placed between the ends of the clamp when the screw is turned into place.

Figs. 5, 6 and 7 show how the spindle may be mounted on a convenient floor stand and driven with a ¼-hp. motor. Fig. 6 suggests a good method of mounting the motor with the shaft in the horizontal position and driving with a half-crossed round leather belt. But, if you have a ball-bearing motor, you can simplify this installation by mounting the motor with the shaft in the vertical position. In either case, with a motor running at 1750 r.p.m., you can use a 7-in. V-pulley on the motor shaft and a 2-in. pulley on the spindle. This combination will give the proper speed for the average work. The stand, as you see, is a very simple affair made from angle iron. The table top requires a little more care. It should be made of strips of hardwood glued together and drawn tight with iron rods threaded at both ends for a nut and washer. For accurate work it's essential that the table top be surfaced

smooth and flat on both sides. Finish it with shellac. Notice the guide pin, Fig. 7, which is necessary for starting the work when no fence is used. It should not be more than 3 in. from the center or axis of the spindle. When using the pin as a guide for the edge of the work in starting the cut, it is essential that the uncut portion of the stock ride on a guide collar as in the detail, Fig. 1. Although the pin can be used when starting either straight or curved work it's best to use a fence when molding straight stock. Fig. 5 suggests a simple type of fence, although it does not have an adjustment for offsetting the two halves which is necessary on certain kinds of work. A ready-made fence having this feature can be purchased at nominal cost. Three-lipped cutters should be used. They may be purchased ready-ground in a great variety of shapes together with suitable guide collars. Always use double nuts on the spindle and be sure that they are tight before starting the machine.

Efficient SCROLLSAW *for Heavy Duty*

A High-Speed Machine with a 22-In. Swing

By A. L. MILLS

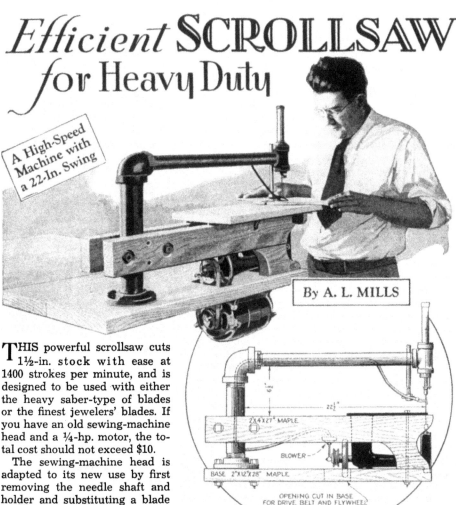

BASE 2"x12"x28" MAPLE

2x4x27" MAPLE

22½"

BLOWER

OPENING CUT IN BASE FOR DRIVE BELT AND FLYWHEEL

THIS powerful scrollsaw cuts 1½-in. stock with ease at 1400 strokes per minute, and is designed to be used with either the heavy saber-type of blades or the finest jewelers' blades. If you have an old sewing-machine head and a ¼-hp. motor, the total cost should not exceed $10.

The sewing-machine head is adapted to its new use by first removing the needle shaft and holder and substituting a blade holder. The head is then inverted and securely bolted between two lengths of 2 by 4-in. maple which are supported on two hardwood blocks bolted either to a separate base or directly to the bench top. Due to variations in the size and needle stroke of different types of sewing-machine heads, slight alterations may be found necessary when assembling, and for this reason some of the dimensions have been omitted as they depend on the particular installation you will use.

Pipe and fittings are used for the frame. When assembling it, the joints should be turned in as tightly as possible. The flange is securely bolted to the base. A saw table of ⅞-in. hardwood is made to fit over and around the base of the sewing-machine head. It is covered with a 10 by 20-in. plate of No. 12-gauge aluminum. A ½-in. hole is drilled in the plate to form an opening for the blade. The upper slide shaft, or plunger, is made from a 9-in. length of ½-in. seamless steel or brass tubing. The lower end is bushed with a piece of brass tubing soldered in place and tapped to take a 1½-in. length of ⅜-in. bolt. The shaft guide is then drilled as shown. It is held against the end of the tubing with a thin nut. A wooden disk,

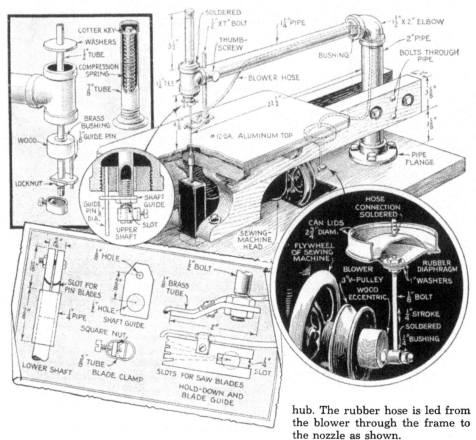

hub. The rubber hose is led from the blower through the frame to the nozzle as shown.

Stepped Bushing Driver Handy For Various Sizes

Sawed from a piece of flat steel, this simple bushing driver is made easily in any size desired. One end is shaped to provide a handle and the other end is sawed in steps, progressively smaller in size. These should be uniform on both sides, and each succeeding step should be about $\frac{3}{16}$ in. smaller than the preceding one. The spacing can be varied, of course, to suit work that occurs most frequently.

bushed with brass to fit the plunger, carries the lower end of the latter and also the metal guide pin which prevents the plunger from turning. The wooden disk is turned into the lower end of the pipe tee.

Other details of the upper-plunger assembly are shown in the drawing.

The combination blade guide and holddown is made by first sawing the head from a $\frac{1}{2}$ by 8-in. carriage bolt and filing two $\frac{1}{8}$-in. grooves in the threaded end at right angles to the length. The end of the hold-down is slotted to fit the grooves and is held with two nuts as shown. Narrow slots are filed in the opposite end of the hold-down to serve as guide slots for the various sizes of blades. The blower nozzle is formed by bending a short length of $\frac{1}{8}$-in. tubing to an elbow. A blower is easily made from tin-can lids and is driven by means of a wooden eccentric attached to the outer end of the V-pulley

Workshop SAW TABLE
is large and sturdy

BUILT with a sturdy angle-iron frame and a laminated hardwood top this motor-driven saw gives you ample capacity for crosscutting and ripping wide boards. The large table is stationary. A novel device for raising and lowering the saw makes it possible to cut to any desired depth within the limits of the saw blade.

The four legs are cut from 1¾-in. angle iron, the top rails from 1½-in. angle iron and the middle stretchers from channel iron, 4 in. wide. Fig. 6 gives you the location of the ⁵⁄₁₆-in. holes to be drilled in each leg. These holes are in the same position on both faces of the angle. The location of the holes through the ends of the rails and stretchers is laid out from those already drilled in the legs. With all holes drilled

you can set up the frame by joining the legs to the channel-iron stretchers with ⁵⁄₁₆-in. stove bolts, the nuts drawn down on lock washers. The top rails are mitered at the ends as in Fig. 5. With the frame set up, drill a line of small holes, spaced 8 in. apart, through the top of the upper angle-iron rails to take screws driven into the top. If the machine is to be taken about to the job or operated on an uneven floor, saw one of the front legs about 1 in. short, cut two ⁵⁄₁₆-in. slots in a piece of ¼ by ¾-in. flat iron and bolt it to the leg as in Fig. 5. This will give you an adjustment to take care of any unevenness in the floor.

The top thickness is given as 1½ in. but this may be 1⅛ in. to allow a greater range

93

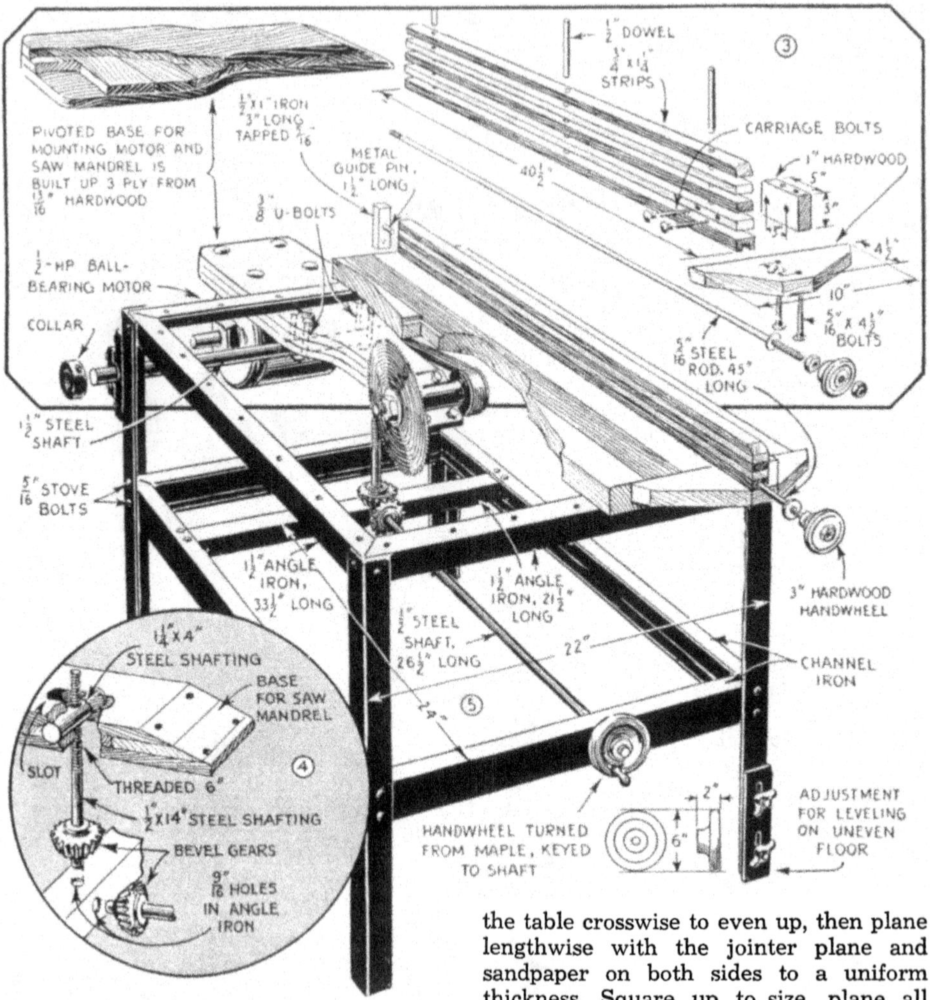

PIVOTED BASE FOR MOUNTING MOTOR AND SAW MANDREL IS BUILT UP 3 PLY FROM 13/16" HARDWOOD
1/2" x 1" IRON 3" LONG TAPPED 5/16
1/2" DOWEL
3/4" x 1 1/4" STRIPS
③
CARRIAGE BOLTS
1" HARDWOOD
5"
3"
METAL GUIDE PIN, 1 1/2" LONG
40 1/2"
3/8" U-BOLTS
4 1/2"
10"
5/16" x 4 1/2" BOLTS
1/2-HP BALL-BEARING MOTOR
COLLAR
5/16" STEEL ROD, 45" LONG
1 1/2" STEEL SHAFT
5/16" STOVE BOLTS
1 1/2" ANGLE IRON, 33 1/2" LONG
1 1/2" ANGLE IRON, 21 1/2" LONG
1/2" STEEL SHAFT, 26 1/2" LONG
22"
24"
⑤
3" HARDWOOD HANDWHEEL
CHANNEL IRON
1 1/4" x 4" STEEL SHAFTING
BASE FOR SAW MANDREL
SLOT
THREADED 6"
④
1/2" x 14" STEEL SHAFTING
BEVEL GEARS
9/16" HOLES IN ANGLE IRON
2"
6"
HANDWHEEL TURNED FROM MAPLE, KEYED TO SHAFT
ADJUSTMENT FOR LEVELING ON UNEVEN FLOOR

of adjustment on the dado and molding heads. To build up the top of 1⅛-in. stock rip six 2¼ by 38-in. strips of hard maple and five strips of black walnut the same size. Run a ⅜ by ¾-in. rabbet on the edge of one of the maple strips. Lay out and drill ⅜-in. holes for staggered 2-in. dowels as shown in Fig. 1. The table opening should be wide enough to take the length of the mandrel so that the saw will raise high enough to give the full cutting capacity of the blade. Cut the stock for the table top accordingly and assemble as in Fig. 1 with waterproof casein glue in all joints. Allow ample time to dry before you loosen the clamps. To finish, first plane the table crosswise to even up, then plane lengthwise with the jointer plane and sandpaper on both sides to a uniform thickness. Square up to size, plane all edges at right angles and be sure that the sides and ends are parallel. Apply two coats of white shellac to both sides and finish with wax. A ⅛-in. rabbet is cut around the top edge of the opening. In this you fit two ⅛-in. steel plates, one slotted for the saw blade, the other with a wider slot for the dado and molding cutter. Fasten with short screws. The ¾-in. groove for the crosscut guide may be located on either side of the saw, or one on each side.

Next you make up the base for the motor and saw mandrel. This is made 3-ply of ¾-in. hardwood. The exact size of the base depends on the type of motor and saw mandrel you use. The forward end of the base is beveled for the mandrel which is usually fastened with bolts or heavy screws. As you will see from Figs. 3 and 6 the base is pivoted on a 1½-in. steel shaft supported in two split bearings bolted to the back legs. The base is attached to the supporting shaft with ⅜-in. U-bolts, or you can use two additional split bearings for this purpose. The motor is bolted in place with a ½-in. V-belt running over a 2-in. diameter V-pulley on the mandrel and a 5-in. V-pulley on the motor. These pulleys will give proper saw speed with the motor turning 1750 r.p.m. This done, you are ready for the tilting device shown in Figs. 4, 6 and 7. It is important that the

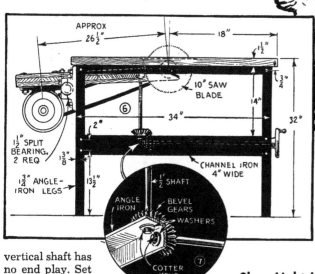

vertical shaft has no end play. Set the table on the frame, align it with the saw blade, place strips of thin felt between the table and the frame, and fasten the table in place with screws.

Fig. 3 details the ripping fence and Fig. 2 the crosscut guide. Both sides of the fence should be finished true throughout the length. The wood is then sanded smooth, shellacked two coats and waxed. Two 1½-in. shaft collars are placed tight against the bearings on the shaft supporting the motor base. All bolts, including those on the split bearings, are then drawn tight. The motor and saw-mandrel mounting, as shown in the drawings, is correct for motors that run in counterclockwise direction as you are facing the pulley. If your motor

runs in clockwise direction, it should be turned end for end so that the pulley and belt are on the opposite side, or the belt may be crossed.

Shop Light Has Clamp-On Socket

When you are working around machinery that requires a light in many unusual positions, it will be a big help to have the lamp fitted with a fastener as shown. This is nothing more than a spring battery clip attached to an ordinary light socket by the bushing screw and then soldered to make it secure.

Albert Mihalovich, Rathbun, Ia.

INDEX

www.ingramcontent.com/pod-product-compliance
Lightning Source LLC
Jackson TN
JSHW011941131224
75386JS00041B/1494